The Sayzeh Song

Junior High's Ups and Downs

An Entirely Different Meaning to Public Education!

by
Chaim B. Segal

DLD Books

ISBN: 1523905603

ISBN–13: 978-1523905607

Note

A glossary of Jewish terms and concepts
is included at the end of this book. It contains all the terms
that will appear in all five books of *The Sayzeh Song*.

Book One

Getting To Know Me

Family Background to Age 14

Introduction

This is the first part of a five-part memoir, in which I wish to describe my overall transition from childhood to adolescence. In this first book, I will describe my own development and that of my immediate family, then describe how I came to perceive the wider world around me. This section will help to set the stage for the succeeding parts of my story. They will focus on learning experiences I gained while attending Stivers, a back-then prominent Dayton City public junior high school. Over the course of the story, I will share how I overcame a number of unexpected physical and emotional obstacles in my transition from childhood to adolescence. I will describe my experiences while traveling, and my enjoyment and perceptions while visiting Washington, D.C., New York City, and Boston for the first time. I will also describe how my overall tastes in music evolved over this time period. Finally, I will describe my quest to understand the cultural differences between myself and the majority of my schoolmates.

Before we begin, I am sure that some of you are wondering what "The Sayzeh Song" is. Well, here's the explanation. Since the 1980s, the use of samplers has become commonplace in popular music, particularly within R&B and dance music. A sampler is used to record one or more musical events, then have them played back and inserted into the music at the touch of a button. Sometimes when the artists or musicians use other enhancing effects, the original words which are fed into the sampler may be distorted, or sound different when heard within the song. In their smash hit song "Say It Isn't So," Daryl Hall and John Oates used a sampler to keep repeating the words "Say It" and "Say It Isn't So" throughout the song at a number of timed intervals. Upon hearing the song for the first time, my brother and I were not used to that style of music. To our untrained ears, it sounded as if a weird voice was calling out the word "Sayzeh!" on a rather frightening-sounding chord. Until the song made a tremendous, lifelong personal impact on me, I thought of it as "The "Sayzeh Song." As will be shown starting in Book Three, that song, "Say It Isn't So," plays a significant role in my story.

Disclaimer

The following story is true. Anything written herein is based solely on my personal opinion and point of view at the time these events were taking place. Nothing said herein regarding members of any ethnic or religious group should be interpreted as denoting any current personal bias on my part. Throughout my five–part story, names of several, but not all, individuals have been changed to protect their character and privacy.

Dedications

I dedicate this memoir to everybody in my life who has helped to shape my personality and state of wellbeing. There are a few who deserve special recognition.

To my dear father, Leon Segal, bless his memory:
I thank you for being there for our family and for teaching me to be an ethically moral person. I apologize for the number of misunderstandings we had.

To my dear mother, Jane Segal:
I thank you for always being there for us and caring for me, even in your old age. I owe many of my life's happiest memories to you.

To my loving wife, Brooke (Hava) Michelle:
I bless our first personal message exchange on Philmore. Thank you for continuing to provide me with a sense of completeness in my life. Through hard times and good times, you are always there for me.

To all three of my older brothers, Chezki (Charlie), Ray, and Moshe:

Thank you for giving me enlightenment when I needed it. Thank you for the good times that I had with each one of you individually.

To my dear Uncle Bob, bless his memory:

Thank you for being my closest relative outside of the family. We still miss your company at family holiday gatherings.

To Joanne and Abe Deutsch, bless their memory:

Thank you for being there as a special force of teaching, loving, and caring throughout my childhood and adolescence. May God continue to raise you high.

To Shelley Hamilton:

Thank you for being a true friend when I most needed one. A major part of this story involves our brief but unique relationship. Our relationship helped me through what was undoubtedly the most trying time in my life.

Finally, to Ms. Annie Bidel, a very special teacher:

I don't know if you are still among us or not. Regardless, thank you for your personal counseling and encouragement when I needed it most. God arranged for us to know each other at just the right time.

Author's Preliminary Words

Over the past hundred years or so, there have been many autobiographical books written by blind people, works that discuss coping with blindness and overcoming both physical and literal obstacles. *The Sayzeh Song* will take a somewhat different tone.

Before I could take on many challenges as a blind adult, there was much that I needed to learn about the wider world in order to understand exactly what things I would need to overcome. In essence, this is the story of some of my most crucial learning experiences.

My time in junior high school was filled with a certain amount of irony. Even now, I am still finding deeper meaning in what happened at the point in time when these events took place.

Over the course of my junior high experience, I would come to recognize how lucky I was in comparison to many other young people, those whose parents had separated or divorced. I would also discover how my interest in music had been slanted by the adults in my life, by my role models. My taste in music would evolve substantially over those years. I would also have a few unique experiences traveling outside of Dayton, proving that a person can derive enjoyment when touring a new place even without the benefit of sight.

A note on the setting: In the early and mid–1980s, the majority of Dayton, Ohio's observant Jewish community lived within the city of Dayton itself. At the time, that was somewhat unusual for a Midwestern city outside of Chicago. I consider the fact that our family resided within the city of Dayton crucial to my story.

Welcome to my first published work. I hope that you can derive both enjoyment and food for thought as you read it.

A hearty and sincere THANKS to you, my readers!
Chaim B. Segal

Chapter 1

My Parents

My ancestors on both sides came from Wilna, Lithuania. This did not matter to me during my early life, but later on, it came up as an interesting fact about our past. I have always thought of our immediate family as American Jewish citizens. However, from the time I was very young, I could sense that we, as a family, were different in some ways from the other Jews and the Gentiles surrounding us.

My father, Leon Saul Segal, was born in Cleveland, Ohio on January 9, 1935. His father was a jewelry salesman whose business required him to do a great deal of traveling. His mother had a vision problem, but for various reasons, she could not seek proper help in dealing with it. Although she was classified as only "legally" blind, her vision problem kept her from working. I think this had an impact on my father.

My father was an only child until he was 12. His parents and he lived in Cleveland until he was about five or six years old. Then his parents relocated to Detroit, where they lived for the next four or five years. Then his parents moved to New York City and set up their home in the Bronx, where my father spent his adolescence. He lived with his parents until he finished high school.

For the most part, the neighborhoods my father's family lived in had many other Jews living in them. It did not matter how religious you were or acted; everyone could enjoy eating corned beef from the deli. Intermarriage between Jews and Gentiles was less common then than it is today. It was more natural for all Jews, regardless of their religious backgrounds, to become friends with and stick with each other in these neighborhoods.

As a young boy, my father was forced to entertain himself for long amounts of time, often with cartoons and comic books. Early on, he had trouble reading text, but he overcame this difficulty during his elementary school years. As he approached high school, he developed various talents and interests. He was quite proud of having been a Tenderfoot in Boy Scouts. In high school, he wrote scripts of plays for his high school theater. I believe that he also wrote songs for the plays.

His mother did not appreciate his talents. Moreover, she did not allow him to join his peers and have similar possessions and interests. For example, when all the other boys his age in their neighborhood had bicycles, she did not allow my father to have one. Her argument was that it wasn't safe. She forced him to throw away a marble collection which had been growing for quite a long time. Although he was very proud of this marble collection, there was nothing he felt he could do or say to persuade his mother to allow him to keep it.

He had been raised with the strong command to obey and respect his parents under all circumstances, regardless of his own feelings. Children were supposed to accept the decisions and standards of their parents at all times. There was absolutely no room for objection. Children also had to accept any type of punishment that their parents might decide to dole out, even when there was a great temptation to fight back. Once, his father spat directly in my father's face. My father could not do anything but take the punishment, living with the memory of the humility for the rest of his life. Little did he realize that generations following his would not put up with similar and harsher punishment, even from parents.

As my father was nearing his teen years, his father's business began to fail. His mother felt that it was her son's duty to provide money for the family to live on. Even if he minded, respect for his mother superseded his own wishes and desires, and he was to be forced into finding work.

Meanwhile, when my father was 12 years old, his younger brother Robert (known to us as Bobby) was born on June 8, 1947. My father had to act as a parent, teacher, and protector to Bobby. As time passed, their parents became increasingly wrapped up in problems of their own regarding the business failure. This was to cause Bobby a major amount of abuse and neglect during his childhood. My father tried his hardest to prevent Bobby from falling victim to this, but unfortunately, that was only possible up to a certain point.

When my father was only 14, his mother suddenly

sent him away from home, telling him not to return until he had a job. After a few days of searching, he managed to find some odd jobs. One of them was as a delivery boy for a fruit store. Much of the money he earned went to pay for Bobby's nursery school.

My father intended to go to college after graduating from high school. He felt with utmost certainty that this would be the only way to raise himself to a higher standard of living than that of his parents. However, he was afraid to leave Bobby at home with their parents, as tension between them was increasing at a steady rate.

At that time, my father's maternal grandmother and his Uncle Sam still lived in Cleveland. Uncle Sam worked as the head of a certain department in a department store. During summer vacations, the family went to Cleveland for visits. My father decided that he wanted to go to college in an area where he had family living. The logical university to be considered was Western Reserve University in Cleveland. His mother fought with him, trying to prevent his going, but she lost. My father paid his own money and took the train from New York to Cleveland to begin his education. His parents joined him there a few years later as the jewelry business finally came to a close.

My mother, Jane Helen Bendow, was born in Brooklyn on April 29, 1937. Her father worked for a company which made parts for printing equipment. This business was somewhat more prosperous than my paternal grandfather's was. Her mother was a nurse, which inspired my mother to try to become one herself at some time in her adult life. However, she never completed her nursing studies. At the time of her birth, she had an older brother, Bruce, who was almost four years older than she was. Her early life was apparently more comfortable than my father's.

When she was four years old, company management relocated her father's job to the mountain town of Hazelton, Pennsylvania, for the duration of World War II. On November 16, 1945, her younger sister, Ellen, was born. As my mother neared her tenth birthday, the family moved back east to Englewood, New Jersey, which is just across the Hudson River from Manhattan. Her family lived there for the rest of her elementary and high school years.

Like my father, my mother and her brother, Bruce, were involved with Scouts. However, Bruce rose to a higher rank than my father in his Boy Scout troop and went on several world jamborees. After joining the service and doing his required duty, Bruce obtained a degree in journalism. He was eventually hired by the United Nations and spent a great portion of his life in Geneva, Switzerland. There, he met and married a German woman named Trauta. Bruce and Trauta had two children, my cousins Julia and Eugene.

After obtaining a teaching degree, my Aunt Ellen eventually married a man named Marty Resnick and moved to Connecticut. She taught first grade for around 40 years. Until much later on, the rest of the family had hardly any chance of getting to know her.

Unlike my father, my mother found it easier to make friends and get along with more people outside of her family. During her school years in Englewood, New Jersey, she made many friends. However, as the years went by, she lost contact with most of them. The one lifelong friendship of hers was with a girl named Suzanne, who later became an artist. After marrying another artist named Adolph Goldman, Suzanne moved to Milwaukee. As a family, we traveled to Milwaukee about 10 times during my childhood to visit the Goldmans, mainly Sue. That's probably why the two names Sue and Milwaukee have always stuck together in my mind.

My mother loved music. When she was only 10 years old, she took the bus across the river into Manhattan by herself to take high–level piano training at The Julliard School of music. Her talents were more respected by her family than my father's were by his family. As a matter of fact, one of the oldest sentimental pieces that we own is a piano which was purchased for my mother by her aunt when my mother was only 10.

Upon my mother's graduation from high school, her parents felt that she should go to college in a different region of the country for an extra cultural experience. For some unknown reason, they decided on her going to Western Reserve University in Cleveland. It was there that my father and she met.

My father had been raised Conservative Jewish. However, his Russian–born maternal grandparents still kept old traditions. His grandfather took him to his Shul from time to time. This exposed him to Orthodox Judaism at a young age. At first, he could not understand why people kept the law in such a strict manner. However, in time, he began to feel that there was much validity in what the people he observed were doing, and he hoped to take on their practices someday when he had a family of his own. Later on, what he had chosen to keep of the traditions through the years gave him a certain stability in other areas of his life.

My mother was raised Reform Jewish, but she felt a godly presence whenever she was around nature. She had always retained good memories of the Reform rabbi in Hazelton, Pennsylvania after she moved away from there. In her day, girls did not have Bat Mitzvahs, but she did not feel deprived of anything. Despite their going to Temple, and then to a Conservative synagogue in Englewood, New Jersey later on, her parents rarely spoke in the home about anything pertaining to religion. Although she attended Sunday school during her growing years, my mother did not learn too much from it. For several years into her life, she did not even know about the existence of Orthodox Judaism.

At the time my parents met at Western Reserve University, there was only one Jewish affiliation which accommodated all levels of religious practice. This was the Hillel House, which held Conservative services on the High Holy Days. My parents met one Yom Kippur at the Hillel House services.

By this point, my father had been a university student for several years and had earned many state teachers' certificates. He had to work during his college years to pay his own tuition. Although he really wanted to be a writer, he settled on obtaining a PhD in psychology. My mother was working toward a degree in social work.

My parents courted for about two years before they married. During this time, my father took her home to his family on weekends. She found the atmosphere in his home very different from that in her own home back in Englewood, New Jersey. Very often, he would leave her to talk to his parents as he retired to his bedroom to sleep off a long week's worth of work and study. His mother was not eager to lose a son to her, but she kept telling my mother that she had no idea how lucky she was to have my father as a husband.

Dad and Mom married in Cleveland on the evening of January 31, 1959. The location arrangements resulted in awkwardness and tension on both sides. Mom's family members feared that she was entering into a lifestyle of less class than she had been brought up with. With the jewelry business having failed, there was certainly a lack of money on Dad's side. Dad's mother felt that it was unfair that their side had to pay for out-of-town relatives to be put up in motels in Cleveland.

The wedding took place in the chapel of an agency where Dad was working at the time. The ceremony was conducted by the same rabbi who had conducted the wedding of Dad's parents; thus he was an extremely old man. Due to his age, he had a health problem which caused him to shake. Years later, Mom would recall with a laugh how he accidentally spilled some of the ceremonial wine on her wedding dress.

Different people compare life to many different things. I would say that life is like an ongoing journey. For my parents, their wedding was the starting point of a very long but interesting section of their journey ahead. All aboard!

Dad had been brought up keeping kosher to a somewhat lenient degree. He intended to keep this practice up and insisted before they married that Mom abide by this. Having grown up with limited knowledge of religious practices, Mom knew absolutely nothing about keeping kosher and what it entailed. However, she was willing to abide by anything Dad set out for her. His mother proceeded to teach Mom how to cook in the way he would eat. Actually, my grandmother kept tabs on this by phone, making sure that Mom was feeding her precious son well. Although she got annoyed with Dad's mother, there was little that Mom could do. The form of eating that my grandmother insisted on was a very costly and unhealthy form of eating. However, for two years, before Dad's mother died of cancer, my parents ate in this manner. At the time, doctors warned Dad to diet, but it was hard for him to do so.

For a while, Dad taught in an inner-city Cleveland school. Then he worked in a place for disturbed people. He was still taking courses in psychology at Western Reserve University in order to become a licensed psychologist anywhere in the country.

Chapter 2

My Brothers

My oldest brother, Charlie, was born on January 29, 1961. My father's parents died within the next few years, and his Uncle Sam would also die at some point in the next eight years. Mom would later tell me that Dad and she moved at least 15 times during the first two years of their marriage before they finally settled down. They lived in Cleveland Heights, Cleveland, Aurora, and Elyria. One of the places in Cleveland where they lived was a trailer house. Dad's mother died during that time. His father died two years later. Being only 14, Bobby was left to be cared for by friends and other relatives most of the time.

In time, Dad got work farther southwest in the state in the Wilburforce area. The family then moved southwest to Yellow Springs, a small, village–like town in Green County. Dad and Mom felt they had no choice but to take Bobby with them and let him be their responsibility. Feeling unfulfilled by his childhood, Bobby was very reluctant to leave Cleveland. He could never feel very comfortable living with Dad, Mom, and Charlie, as nothing could be 100 percent the way his mother had made it.

Soon after the move to Yellow Springs, about four years after Charlie was born, my second-oldest brother, Ray, was born on November 4, 1964. At that time, one of Dad's former advisors from college invited him back to Cleveland to finish work which would enable him to receive his PhD, which he had never officially received. Being totally sick and tired of schoolwork, and with a growing family to support, Dad did not have a desire to do this and declined the offer. In my opinion, this was a serious mistake, and it set the tone of my tale that follows.

Toward the end of the family's years in Yellow Springs, my third oldest brother, Moshe, was born on August 28, 1966. It appeared to Dad and Mom that his development was somewhat abnormal. The doctors insisted that nothing whatsoever was wrong with him. It took them 16 months to diagnose that he was, at the very least, legally blind.

Around that time, Dad was doing more work for Central State University, a state-supported university adjacent to Wilburforce University. Both universities are made up of predominantly black students and faculty.

Dad and Mom were friends with a Jewish couple in Yellow Springs who later divorced on account of religion. The woman was inspired to become religious by Shlomo Carlebach, "The Singing Rabbi," who came to perform at Antioch University (located in Yellow Springs). She moved with her children to Boro Park.

When Charlie was 10, this woman invited him to come up and spend Shavuos (or Shavuot) with her. He stayed for a number of weeks afterwards and became totally drawn into the lifestyle there. Just before his return, the woman warned him not to try to uphold this lifestyle while living with our parents. She warned him that it might not be possible for him to do as she was doing because our parents would not be able to provide for it.

Charlie was won over, however, and he became adamantly religious. For a period of a few years after this, he went to religious camps every summer. Life at home was becoming more and more complicated as Charlie insisted that the family try to abide by religion in a strict manner. Dad and Mom did not adopt all observances at that time, but Dad felt that he should listen to Charlie to a certain extent. I am not sure why he did not maintain better control of the situation. Mom herself was becoming inspired and tried to do much of what Charlie said. However, with there being very few Jews in Wilburforce and Xenia, this was not easy.

When Moshe was about two years old, the family moved to Xenia after living in the Wilburforce area for about a year. Mom would later claim that our family was happiest of all living in Yellow Springs and did not know how much they were going to miss living there.

Bobby graduated from Yellow Springs High School about the time the family moved to Wilburforce. Discontented with living with Dad and Mom, he decided to move back to the old house in Cleveland instead of going away to a special school to study radio broadcasting. Allowing himself to become haunted by old memories, he developed serious, lifelong emotional problems. He learned clarinet and eventually played professionally. Also, he did not go to college right away. If I remember correctly, it was Dad who got him set up in college. He later became a teacher in the Cleveland public school system. He played clarinet and acted as a clown on the side.

The family lived in Xenia approximately two or three months before I was born. I, Chaim Baruch, was born on Tuesday, October 29, 1968 at 5:15 a.m. in Kettering Hospital. Four months later, it was confirmed that I too would be blind, or at least severely visually impaired for life. Being the two fine people Dad and Mom were, they realized right away that Moshe and I still had the ability to carry on normal lives, as many blind people had throughout history.

At the time, Dad and Mom were considering taking on more religious observances. They were now driving in from Xenia on Saturday mornings to attend Shabbos services at Beth Abraham synagogue—which, by that time, was Conservative. They were also driving Charlie and Ray to Sunday school at Beth Abraham each and every Sunday during the school year. Apparently, from what I've been told, I screamed throughout the entire trip to Dayton and back.

When I was two years old, a test was given to Moshe in Columbus at the Ohio State School for the Blind to evaluate his mental capacity. Moshe was only four years old at the time, but he was well aware of what was going on around him. The first thing that the psychologist who tested him did was tell him, "I'm your uncle." Moshe, of course, knew better, and he made an instantaneous decision to not cooperate with the rest of the testing. Instead, he wandered around the halls of the school, feeling the walls, which displayed interesting art work done by the students. The outcome of his tests showed that he had "a mental problem"—or so they thought.

Dad and Mom knew this was not so, but they were not at a state where they could stand up for themselves. They were shocked and dismayed to receive a notification that Moshe had been enrolled at the School for the Blind by the State of Ohio without their consent. They realized that they had to flee the area in a hurry. This, combined with the desire to take on more religious practices, forced them to move to Dayton in the fall of 1971.

Chapter 3

At Home in Dayton

Finally, when I was nearly three years old, we moved into Dayton View, a section of North Dayton. It was around then that Dad and Mom became interested in Beth Jacob Synagogue. There were a few people who belonged to that synagogue who were rather more observant than most. The rabbi of the synagogue, Rabbi Samuel Fox, helped Dad and Mom find the top section of a duplex across the street and six houses up from the back of Beth Jacob. Our address was 1366 Cory Drive.

Our "house," as we thought of it, had a front door and a back door. The front door was ours alone, with two staircases to get up to our living quarters. We shared the basement, back door, and front porch of the property with our downstairs neighbors. We had a large attic which was accessed via a staircase in back. This attic had two rooms in it, with an abundance of space. Mom stored holiday dishes and extra odds and ends in the attic. The attic eventually became Charlie's bedroom. We also had a balcony all to ourselves. In later years at this address, we slept out on the balcony in the summertime, and in the fall, Dad built a sukkah on it for Sukkos.

At the time we moved in, the Goodmans, an Orthodox Jewish family, were living in the apartment below us. The father and husband was principal of the fairly recently started Hillel Academy. I have almost no memory of this family. At that time, we were alternating between two synagogues. On some Shabbos mornings, we would walk to services at Beth Abraham. Other weeks, we would attend services at Beth Jacob.

Although Dad could not remember every single tradition that he had learned about from his grandfather, there were highlights which stuck out. One of these was the religious fervor which is displayed by thousands of Orthodox Jews each year on Simchat Torah. Dad found the atmosphere in both synagogues lacking on Simchat Torah. He told Mom that the Orthodox synagogues kept the right type of spirit. Mr. Goodman convinced Dad and Mom to come with his family to Shomrei Emuna one Simchat Torah and bring us children along. Thus began our association and affiliation with Congregation Shomrei Emuna: by that time, the only truly Orthodox Jewish synagogue in Dayton, Ohio.

Apparently, even after all this time, Dad still missed his family. Somehow, the memory of going to Shul with his grandfather stuck out in his mind, to the point that he felt that the Shul itself could take the place of the deceased relatives, that it could provide an extended family of sorts. It took many years of attending there for him to realize that this could not be the case. However, I doubt that anything else in Dayton, Ohio or anywhere else could have satisfied his needs and wants.

To the best of my knowledge, Shomrei Emuna was an outgrowth of activities by men from Beth Abraham and Beth Jacob who gave of themselves and walked down to the Jewish Old Folks Home, which was located in Dayton View, in order to help make Shabbos morning services. Then a few involved families decided to start an official Shul and gave a lot of what they had to do it. I will not mention names, because I do not know specifically who these people were. I only know Congregation Shomrei Emuna for what it was during the course of my youth and early adult life.

At one time, Shomrei Emuna was located in a family's basement, where members met for Shabbos services, before buying a house to have as the Shul. The Shul had since gone through many phases, nine rabbis, and many members. In the early fall of 1991, the Shul expanded its property, which had existed for around 16 years in a simple, ordinary house on Salem Avenue, a main street in Dayton. When Dad and Mom first took me to services there, they were located in a house at the corner of Cornell and Catalpa.

Eventually, the Goodmans moved out from below us, and another religious family moved in. This was the Ranan family, consisting of a rabbi named Yisrael, his wife, Naomi, and two sons, Naphtali and Rami. From the start, our two families clicked into friendship. However, with the exceptions of eating Shabbos lunch with them and sharing a sukkah during Sukkos, my memories of our interaction with the Ranans during my younger days are not detailed.

I do remember that for some reason, I was fascinated by Naomi's phone book, which opened at the press of a button. For a short period of time, I would frequently walk downstairs and borrow it from Naomi to play with it. I would do that until I became bored with it, then make my way back upstairs and home. Eventually I broke it, and from then on, she did not allow me to play with it anymore.

I've been told that I still did a lot of screaming in those days.

Rabbi Ranan always enjoyed playing Jewish music for Moshe and me. He also enjoyed sharing small amounts of beer with Moshe. To this day, I have no idea why Dad and Mom let this go on. Rabbi Ranan also owned a vicious German Shepherd named King. One day, King hurt Ray very badly. Although Rabbi Ranan apologized, the incident left a big scar in Ray's mind. Rabbi Ranan's wife eventually kicked him out of the house. She and her children moved to Cincinnati while I was still quite young.

With the exception of a birthday cake and candles for my second or third birthday, as well as moments during swimming outings at the YMCA in Xenia on Saturday nights, my first major memory is from when I was three. This is of a shopping errand Dad took me on one Friday afternoon. Throughout my life, he always took a great amount of pride in shopping for Shabbos. Given my stage of development at the age of three, he would often take me with him on Friday afternoons to get me out of Mom's hair, so that she could prepare the house for Shabbos. On this particular Friday that I remember so clearly, he was in an unusually good mood. As he wheeled the shopping cart through the supermarket, he was humming almost continuously. Every so often, he would call me by an affectionate nickname, such as "Piechicle" or "Fagela." He also made up silly songs, using my name time and again.

Chapter 4

Early School Days

I began Hillel Academy Nursery about a year before the Ranan family moved to Cincinnati. My overall memories of Hillel Academy Nursery are pleasant. I remember that every Friday, they had what was known as "Shabbat." The entire nursery class said the traditional blessings over wine and bread, and we drank grape juice and ate challah. To me, the experience seemed like a watered–down version of what we had that night and next day around a large table in the dining room as a family.

I adored the nursery school teacher, Mrs. Sloan. I always wanted to bring her things. One Shabbos morning, a brand new box of Dad's checks was sitting on the table, waiting to be used or filed. Not thinking that my actions could be a problem, I picked up the box of checks and began to turn it over and over in my hands. Mom had told me prior to this that checks were money. I did not know that what I was holding was a box of checks, until Charlie called out, "Hey, Mom, Chaim has Dad's checks. You'd better take them away from him." Upon hearing that what I was holding in my hands was a box of checks, I became even more possessive of it, hugging the box against myself, planning to bring it to school with me to give to Mrs. Sloan.

The tighter I held the box, the louder Charlie began to yell. Finally, Mom stepped in from the kitchen and snatched the box of checks away from me as I began to cry. As I wailed that I wanted to give them to Mrs. Sloan, because they were money, Mom began to laugh. I did not think it was the slightest bit funny, and Mom promptly pacified me with a piece of candy.

I remember only one time when I needed to be disciplined at nursery school. This was when I hit a girl over the head with a music box after she had taken a long time to finish playing with it. The punishment was not severe and was soon out of my mind after I left the building for the day.

I was in the Hillel Academy Nursery for two years. During the second year, we students had our mothers come in on our birthdays to help us celebrate. In some ways, I think that my two years in nursery school were the happiest school years of my life.

After my second year of nursery school, I was switched to Grant School, a public elementary school on Dayton's east side, where I attended the preschool for the Blind and Visually Handicapped of Dayton and surrounding communities. I was in preschool for two years. Our teacher was known to us as Mrs. B. She could be a fun woman to have as a teacher, but she could be quite frightening when it came to punishment. When somebody did something wrong, even when it was a total accident and not really the fault of the wrongdoer, the person was put in the time-out chair. If crying persisted, she would make the child stand for over an hour. We students tried our hardest to avoid the time-out chair, but some of us could not be so lucky.

Mrs. B. made a big deal about a child eating everything on his or her lunch plate or tray, especially if it was brought from home. She used the time-out chair as a means of punishment should a child not eat. One day at lunch time, I discovered to my horror that Mom had packed a tuna fish sandwich in my lunch. In my entire life, I have never liked the taste of tuna fish once it has come in contact with bread. When I refused to eat the sandwich, Mrs. B. put me in the time-out chair, where I sat and cried for a long while.

I had begun to forget why I was sitting there when she walked over and commanded me to stand against a locker. She left me standing there for what felt like an endless amount of time. Growing tired, I began to lean against the locker, until she demanded that I stand straight. Finally, probably at the suggestion of one of the aides in the classroom, she let me resume normal activities, but she continuously begged me to eat the sandwich. If I remember correctly, the last thing she said to me that day before my departure from school was, "When you get home, eat that sandwich!" To this day, I will still not eat a tuna fish sandwich if I have a more desirable option.

Around this time at home, I was becoming more conscious than ever before of space around me. When nothing else was going on that directly involved or affected me, I felt a need to be in constant motion, especially whirling around and around in circles. Dad and Mom would both yell at me, telling me, "Stop twirling!" I would listen for the time being, but would then forget about having been yelled at for doing this.

Eventually, Dad began to act as if my twirling was a major offense, and he adopted harsher measures of punishment for it. One Friday night in the middle of winter, after everyone else had gone to sleep, I found my way out of bed and into the kitchen, where I began turning around in circles. I figured that I would just turn around and around all night, and there would be no problem. Instead, Dad came out of his bedroom and saw me. Without a word, he lifted me off my feet, held me in mid–air, and began to spank me without saying anything. He carried me to my bedroom and inserted me in bed. Making sure that everything else was okay, he left the room. I fell asleep in minutes. However, this event did not stop me from twirling.

Late one afternoon a few months later, Moshe and I were alone in the house with Dad, who was seemingly busy. Having a lot of energy, I felt a need to dissipate it. I began turning circles in the main hall of our home, when Dad suddenly appeared on the scene. Bending me over, he began to spank me harder than I could remember ever having been spanked before. I had not realized that any man could hit a person so hard. The spanking went on and on. At one point, Dad pounded a spot on me which made me urinate in my pants. He began to rave, over and over again, about how bad and wrong it was for me to twirl, saying that I could get very sick by doing this. I did not understand what the big deal was, but now I feared that I would somehow get into additional trouble, having just peed in my pants. I forget how this instance resolved itself, but a repeat ensued a few months later in the middle of the summer.

I retained this unfortunate twirling habit for a few years longer. What finally made me give it up was simply losing the urge to do it any longer. Perhaps it's no wonder that in my younger days, my favorite amusement park ride was the Tilt–a–Whirl. As far as I can see, the most notable damage the habit did me was that it caused me to socially isolate myself from other people my age in play at school and in other places.

The incident of urinating in my pants when I was being spanked left an internal scar which I was not to discover until years later. In the few years that followed, I developed a fascination with urine. That turned into a fear of it when I began to have bad dreams which ended in my wetting the bed.

In school at one point, Mrs. B. had just read the story of "The Three Billy Goats Gruff" to the class. She tried to make herself sound especially frightening as she imitated the troll. Not long after she had finished reading the story and had begun another class activity, I became aware that I was feeling good. In a feeling of pure pleasure, I began to move my body around as I sat on the floor with the rest of the class. I had no idea that I was bothering anybody; I was probably only bothering one person.

Next thing I knew, though, Mrs. B. walked over to me and yanked me up from the floor. Taking me to the time-out chair, she scolded, "It looks like somebody's going to get eaten. You'd better be good, or the troll will come and get you." Although I was six years old at the time, I believed her. That night, I had a hard time falling asleep and had to sleep in Dad and Mom's bed for comfort.

Every day in preschool, there was a period of time just after lunch known as "sleep rest." Anybody who was not in the time-out chair was supposed to lie on the floor and sleep, or at the very least, be quiet as two children's records were played.

We went on several field trips during my two preschool years. I turned five during my first year of preschool and six during my second. Neither year was more exciting than the other, but the second year was slightly more eventful.

Chapter 5

More About School

Charlie and the Yeshiva

Charlie's Bar Mitzvah occurred during January following my fifth birthday. Notably, it was the first Bar Mitzvah to have ever taken place in Shomrei Emuna. Because Charlie had not attended Sunday school or Hebrew school in the community for the required amount of time, the policies held by all authorities prohibited Dad and Mom from having his Bar Mitzvah at Beth Abraham or Beth Jacob.

I remember mounting excitement in the house before the affair and Mom being very busy. I did not realize that Charlie was the reason for the excitement until I found myself in Shomrei Emuna that Shabbos morning in the midst of a massive crowd. As the Torah was being read, someone walked by me and handed me two hard candies. One was a favorite of mine at the time, a sesame candy. Meanwhile, I heard Charlie reading from the Torah, but I didn't understand exactly what was happening or what the significance was. Without thinking about it, I ate the candies, but the person who had given them to me had assumed I knew that they were to be thrown at Charlie. All of a sudden, Charlie stopped chanting and a whole bunch of people began throwing candy at him. For a second, I felt bad that I had not saved my candy to throw at Charlie. However, I had to admit to myself that it had tasted good, and I was glad I had not missed it.

I don't remember much else about the celebration. Apparently, a party was given at Hillel Academy by Dad and Mom the night after the service, but I slept through that back at home.

Charlie's Bar Mitzvah was more than just the first Bar Mitzvah of Shomrei Emuna; it also started another Dayton custom. Throughout Jewish history, candy had only been thrown in synagogues at grooms at an Aufrauf. Apparently, somebody thought it would be a neat and colorful idea to do it at Charlie's Bar Mitzvah. Guests who were members of Beth Abraham and Beth Jacob who were in Shomrei Emuna that morning thought it was a splendid idea. It later became common practice in every synagogue in Dayton, with the exception of the Reform ones, to throw candy at Bar and Bat Mitzvahs after the respective person had his or her first Aliyah.

At home during this time, Charlie was constantly urging Mom and Dad to send him to a Yeshiva. Dad wrote a letter to the Lubavitcher Rebbe explaining the dimensions of our family and his livelihood, asking the Rebbe for a recommendation for Charlie. The Rebbe wrote back, stating that Dad should move the entire family to a larger

Jewish community rather than send Charlie by himself. The Rebbe explained to Dad that with our family's special circumstances, we would be better off in a larger area where we could find other families with similar circumstances, among whom we would be comfortable.

Although the Rebbe did not name a particular location, Dad and Mom figured that the New York area was what he had in mind. Knowing the cost of living in New York City or any area nearby, Dad thought and insisted that it would be virtually impossible for us to live there comfortably. Mom thought it could work, and she was trying her hardest to raise Moshe and me to be prepared to live the lifestyle of Orthodox Jews. When she could, she obtained Jewish music for us—a lot of which was Chasidic music. She tried her hardest to encourage the two of us to learn every single song on every Jewish record by heart, telling me that soon we would be living among people with whom I would sing those songs around tables. I could not understand what she was trying to say to me, but I did manage to learn several of the melodies.

At the end of my first year of preschool, Mom and Charlie traveled to the New York area together by Greyhound bus to look for a Yeshiva. That fall, Charlie enrolled in one in Far Rockaway.

Between my two years of preschool, the family took a car trip down to Miami, Florida to visit Mom's relatives who had moved down there. It took three days to travel each way. On one of the nights on our way down, we drove straight through the night. If I remember correctly, I woke up that morning and was told by Charlie or Ray that we were in Georgia and that Mom was driving the car, so I could not talk to her. It was usually Dad who took the wheel for most long trips.

Throughout our stay in Florida each time, we stayed in a hotel which was directly off the beach. Mom's father had paid for us, as well as her brother and his family, to come spend some time there. On this first trip, I was a little too young to have much fun, but I enjoyed my grandfather and step-grandmother fussing over me. One of the first things we did on arrival was to walk out into the ocean. I was frightened by it and did not go out there much more after that first experience. On our way back, we stopped off in Tennessee, where Mom and Dad made Shabbos in a trailer motel. We also stopped in Kentucky the following day and visited Mammoth Caves. My main memory of these caves is that they were cold and involved a lot of steps.

My second year of preschool was no better or worse than the first. That year, I rode to and from school by bus. It was on the bus that I started to become buddies with a classmate who was about six weeks younger than I was. His name was Matthew Chaney, or Matt, and he lived in a nearby town called Bellbrook.

During this year, I attended regular kindergarten for a large part of the afternoon. I found it boring and seldom wanted to attend. When it was time to go there, I often fought Mrs. B. by sticking out my tongue at her, which only resulted in a seat in the time-out chair. By the end of the year, however, I had come to enjoy kindergarten. I had discovered that I liked many of the activities that Mrs. Johnson, the teacher, initiated.

This was also the year that I began to learn Braille. To do so, I was taken by a preschool aide to Moshe's classroom. The teacher in that classroom was Mrs. Wilkinson. I found her to be a good teacher, one who made sure I was learning the Braille that she was trying to teach me. When she had other things to do in order to teach her class, she would have other students of hers work with me. Eventually, she had Moshe and me work together.

In May of that year, my preschool and the kindergarten combined in order to have a televised Mayday celebration. At the tail end of the show, I sang the song "Sunrise, Sunset" from *Fiddler on the Roof* into a microphone. Many staff members in the school were proud of me, despite the fact that I sang most of the words to the song wrong, as I learned later on.

I believe it was this school year that I began piano lessons with JoAnn Basch. As I will detail later, she did our family a great many favors in her time. We also shared many happy occasions.

For the next two school years, I was moved upward to Mrs. Wilkinson's class. This class was a primary unit for blind and visually impaired pupils in the first, second, and third grades. My experiences with Mrs. Wilkinson differed from the previous year. As her official pupil, I found her to be strict, but equally willing to offer rewards for good work and good behavior. Her usual method of discipline consisted of sending a disorderly student out into the hallway for about 10 minutes. Sometimes that person would also have to eat his or her lunch in the classroom, away from the rest of the class. During my first year in her class, there was a party just about every Friday for all the pupils who had maintained good behavior and had put forth their best effort all week long. During that year, most of us students were on the same learning level.

That year, Moshe was in Mr. Brinkman's class; he taught the higher level students in our position. For some reason, Ray was also attending Grant School that year. He was in the regular fifth grade class.

The previous year, Mom had worried a lot about Charlie, who was attending the Yeshiva in Far Rockaway. Charlie had been sleeping in a dormitory which was set up for college students. Although the other students invited him out for a good time, he chose to keep to himself and was left alone much of the time. Once, he was invited to come into Brooklyn on a Saturday night and got mugged on a subway train on his way back to the dormitory. In addition to this, he had to carry his dirty laundry five blocks to get to where he could wash it. Although Charlie survived the mugging, it became evident to Mom that she could not bear to have him that far from home. Thus arrangements had been made for him to attend Telshea Yeshiva near Cleveland the following year.

Telshea Yeshiva (the name is pronounced "Telz") is one of the strictest Yeshivas in the world. People from all over the world study there. The religious learning is very intense and not for everybody—even for many students from homes where there was even more religious observance than in our home. When the Yeshiva transplanted itself from Europe, the head rabbis chose to set up in locations such as the Midwest, where there needs to be a massive force to act as a generator of serious Judaic learning and practice. Knowing our background, the Telshea rabbis tried to convince Dad and Mom that Charlie would not do well in Telshea. But Dad and Mom were certain that Charlie had to attend Yeshiva closer to home.

Charlie lasted only one year at Telshea. We visited him during winter vacation. I was too young to realize how isolated the Yeshiva campus was from the rest of Cleveland. We spent Shabbos in their adjoining guest house and did not have a very pleasant experience. The rabbis there pushed Charlie and the other students to obey religious law in a stricter manner than anything Charlie had ever experienced.

In their own ways, the guys fought back. After the main rabbi on duty slammed the door of the dorm room for the night, ignoring those students who seemed to be having a problem, he would go on his way as the guys got their hidden life in. Charlie told me years later of how he would get out of bed and lift weights, and also how another roommate would take out a Sony radio with headphones and gleefully listen to his favorite music.

Charlie began to suffer in this atmosphere, especially when a window in his room got broken and nobody in charge did anything about it. Eventually, he began to sneak away from Telshea on his bicycle to check books out of the Cleveland Public Library. (No literature outside of Judaic literature, including the daily newspaper, was allowed in Telshea.) Charlie was almost caught by one of the main rabbis, who pretended not to have seen him in the library.

Finally, it became too much for Charlie, who carried on

a private rebellion by fasting for three days straight. When the head rabbis found out about this and other activities that Charlie was involved in, they contacted Dad and Mom to tell them not to send Charlie back there the following year. Meanwhile, Moshe and I had absolutely no idea how much Charlie was suffering at Telshea. When he would come home for vacation, we would always tease him, telling him, "Go back to Telz." For the most part, he kept his suffering to himself when he was at home.

Chapter 6

Alvin, Music, and Problems at Home

Up until this point, I had always taken it for granted that we owned a medium–size dog named Alvin. He was actually Bobby's dog, named after Alvin the Chipmunk. That year, he grew more and more senile as the school year progressed. At age 19, he lost his hearing and sense of space. Mom had to go downstairs with him at 4:00 a.m. to take him outside so he could relieve himself; cancer and arthritis had caused him to be too weak to go out by himself. One Sunday morning, Mom took him outside the house as I was leaving to go somewhere. Alvin disappeared, and that evening, Mom and Dad informed us that he was dead.

During my two years in the primary unit, I developed a crazy infatuation with anything that made music. No matter where I was or what was going on around me in any situation, I was finding every opportunity possible to talk to any single person about music boxes and musical toys. At home, the entire family became weary of my talking about the subject and demanded time and again that I stop. I took this to mean that everybody at home, especially Mom and Dad, thought I was some sort of jerk, despite all the love they still gave me.

Although current affairs really did not mean very much to me, something did happen during my first year of Mrs. Wilkinson's class, in 1976, which left an impression on me. There was much programming that year in school pertaining to the Bicentennial. I did not understand our country's celebration of 200 years of existence. However, I liked the various plays and musical performances in school in honor of this event.

It was at this point in my life that it began to matter to me whether a person was white or black. It all began when I discovered that certain people whom we met and talked to outside of our home had a different way of speaking than we did. I was also becoming aware of a not–so–nice term used by Jews to talk about various people on the street. I finally figured out that it was most blacks who had a different way of pronouncing their words than we did, and I began to ask Mom if various people we knew were white or black. When she told me that Mrs. Wilkinson was black, I did not believe her, because her whole way of talking and speaking to our class did not resemble the speech of other people on the street who were notably black.

Unfortunately, I had to learn a hard lesson about this matter. One Shabbos afternoon, the entire family, with the exception of Dad and Charlie (who was in Yeshiva), were taking a Shabbos walk through the neighborhood when two or three black teenagers said "Hi" to us. On the spot, I asked Mom if they were black. She firmly put her hand over my mouth and hit me very hard. She went on yelling at me for five minutes straight as we terminated the walk. I felt guilty for my wrongdoing for a few days, then forgot about the incident until a certain point within this story. After that incident, I came to the conclusion that there were both white and black people who were no different from one another, except for the fact that we supposedly had reason to fear some blacks. However, there was still another lesson on this matter for me to learn about four years later.

That summer, Mom, Charlie, Ray, Moshe, and I flew to Miami, Florida to visit Mom's father and our step-grandmother once again. That was the first airplane trip that I can remember taking. The experience of flying was not what I had expected. I found the flight itself to be boring, and I had a tremendous earache in both ears as the plane landed. Fortunately, Mom had an ample amount of chewing gum to give us. That was to keep us swallowing, to combat the air pressure.

As was the case the previous trip, Uncle Bruce and Aunt Trauta came with our cousins Julia and Eugene. I had a much better time on that trip than I had had two years before. I especially liked it when Grandma took me to a toy store and bought me a Fisher Price Music Box Record Player. Although I was still somewhat afraid of the ocean, Mom kept encouraging me to leave the hotel to spend more time in the water. She finally realized that I was too young to comprehend that this was a special body of water. We were a little sad to leave Florida but felt refreshed by our vacation.

Later that summer, between my years in Mrs. Wilkinson's class, Charlie and Ray took a long trip with Dad to Washington, D.C. and Baltimore. Upon their return, they told me that Charlie would be going to a Yeshiva in Baltimore the upcoming school year. I had never heard of Baltimore before and wondered what kind of city it was.

That September, my second and final year in Mrs. Wilkinson's class began. This school year was slightly more eventful, both inside and outside of school, than the previous year. On each successive vacation visit home that school year, Charlie brought home two brand new Jewish records for Moshe and me. As glad as he always was to see us, we could sense a greater bitterness in his attitude each time he came home. He returned home for the summer a few days after Grant School ended for the year.

As I was riding with Mom and him in the car on some errands, he suddenly got into a very emotional discussion with Mom about his future. When Mom began to offer to send him back to Far Rockaway, he began to kick the floor of the station wagon very hard, shouting, "I don't wanna go back to Yeshiva!" That astonished both Mom and me. A few weeks later, he took a job at a nearby Wendy's; that lasted for a few months. Then he found work at Friendly's. That job lasted nearly an entire year, until he quit. It was at this time that he learned how to drive.

My second year in Mrs. Wilkinson's class was the first

year that I ever participated in a school candy sale. During the fall, I went door to door in our neighborhood, accompanied by Mom, taking orders from people who wanted to buy candy. I could not understand why, but Mom felt somewhat uncomfortable about my doing this. Ray and Moshe also sold candy. One of the prizes for having sold a minimal amount was permission to attend a live rock concert at school. I had already won a Grant School T-shirt, and I decided to attend the rock concert, even though I really did not like that style of music. I figured that if this was a concert, whoever was making the music was likely to make good music.

Grant School always used their gymnasium as a lunch room and auditorium. When I walked into the auditorium the afternoon of the rock concert, I was expecting to hear loud music during the concert, but thought that it would have some type of fun sound to it. Even before the concert, I was to have a bit of a surprise. I was unaware that before the music began, they were going to honor the people who had sold the most candy. Some people thought they needed to announce loudly and clearly to the world who the winners were. However, any normal talk into the microphone emerged from the stage at an unnaturally loud volume. Thus, even before the concert, a few of my classmates who had been eligible to attend the concert began to literally cry to Mrs. Frech, the aide, to take them back to the classroom. I myself had become rather sorry that I had chosen to attend this raucous event, but I decided to try to stick it out.

One of my classmates, Jimmy Mullins, had sold more

candy than anybody else in the school. They honored him onstage before the concert and awarded him $50 and a brand new TV set.

Finally, the concert began. Somebody led me down out of the auditorium bleachers onto the gymnasium floor and told me I could dance. I walked around the perimeter of the gym, not knowing what to make of this horrible racket. What I was hearing hardly resembled music at all. It sounded like a loud, jarring sound with people screaming along with it. I could not hear any rhythmic beat within the noise that even suggested dancing. I could barely understand any spoken or sung word. Eventually, a staff member began to take note of me and sensed that I was truly not enjoying myself. She offered to take me back to Mrs. Wilkinson's classroom, and I happily left the gym with her. I could have gone back by myself, but I didn't know if I was allowed to, given that I had decided to attend the concert. I left the gym with ringing ears and a sore throat that lasted on into the night.

Back in her classroom, Mrs. Wilkinson had arranged a party of sorts for those who were not eligible to attend the rock concert. It was not over by the time I returned. As I sat through a children's movie about a person with suction–cup shoes, I could still hear the band playing from the gym, which was on the other side of the building. I wondered why on earth the band musicians felt they had to play so loudly if they were right in the room with their audience. Finally, the band stopped playing toward the end of the school day. I vowed after that that I would have nothing to do with rock music for the rest of my life. As we will soon see, that vow did not end up being hard and fast, although I had to do some self-educating on this matter at a more reasonable listening level in years ahead.

Meanwhile, as the rest of the family members were still keeping religion in the strict manner that he had led us to, Charlie was suddenly becoming looser and looser in his own practices. Ray, who had displayed signs of desiring serious, strict religious practice, began to loosen up also. The following school year, Charlie attended nearby Fairview High School, and he graduated the following June.

During my second year in Mrs. Wilkinson's class, the country was going through an energy shortage. In order to save heat, Dad demanded that we all sleep together in the same bedroom. Sometimes, Mom would have to bring mattresses to the attic, where we would all sleep for a few nights. Other times, we slept on the floor of Dad and Mom's bedroom. I resented being awakened as other family members finally came into the room for the night. I was glad when that winter was over, as I very much disliked this manner of living.

Meanwhile, Moshe had gradually transferred schools, eventually attending Hillel Academy, where he was placed in the fourth-grade class. There a long-standing promise that I would also be transferred after another year or two. Mom kept telling me that the officials in charge of Grant School were pleading with her not to take me out. She explained to me that there were special skills which were now being taught to the blind that Moshe had never had the chance to learn. Thus I would remain a student at Grant School for the next four years.

Chapter 7

Dad, Charlie, and Other Family Members

Around that time, I realized that Dad's personality was changing at home. Previously, he had enjoyed taking all of us out for fun activities, followed by treating us to ice cream. Now he was still taking us swimming, but he always seemed to be in a rush to come and go. At home, he began to get into more and more arguments with Mom about money. There were other personality changes as well. Very often, especially on Friday afternoons before Shabbos, he would speak to all of us brothers, especially Moshe and me, in a tone of voice that made us feel menaced, telling us that we were constantly doing him wrong. On some occasions, Charlie (when he was around) and Ray would have to call Moshe and me aside and counsel us on how to behave. Problems of this sort were not come and go; they became day-to-day routine after a certain point.

Sometimes at night when I was having a hard time

falling asleep, I would get up and walk out into the dining room just to walk around. As he was busy working in the dining room at his typewriter with the television on, Dad interpreted this behavior as a ploy to gain attention. Instead of trying to encourage me to go back to bed right away, he felt he had to scare me into it, as if I was committing a cardinal sin by being up. It was not enough for him to simply recommend that I go back to bed. He often decided that the best way to handle the situation was to make a terrific issue about it. He would pull me over to a chair or couch in the living room and seat me there. He would then yell at me, telling me that I had to stay there for the entire night—even after he himself went to sleep.

Ironically, his method worked. After about 20 minutes of crying and feeling guilty, I began to get tired. Then, just as I believed that he would actually keep me there the entire night, he released me to go back to bed. Sleep usually came minutes later. However, the next day at school, I could still feel his angry vibrations.

When I asked Mom about this behavior, which I felt was crazy, all she said was that Dad was tired and worked very hard. I had no idea how fortunate I was in comparison to several other students at school, in that I had two parents who had stayed together for as long as mine had. In addition, I probably could not have comprehended how much money my father made in comparison to how much money was in the homes of the other students. To me, it seemed as though everybody's father worked, and most likely worked hard. I could not understand why Dad felt he had to do what he did just because I could not fall asleep.

It was during the second year of Mrs. Wilkinson's class that my maternal grandfather died. With the exception of Uncle Bobby, I had known my grandfather better than any other relative outside of our immediate family. However, I could only recall the two visits we had had with him as a family down in Miami, and once or twice when he had come to Dayton for a short stay.

He died on the second day of Shavuos; I was informed of this within two hours after the holiday ended. When he died, I did not cry because he had passed away, but because Mom was about to go to Florida for a week. Until shortly after my tenth birthday, I always feared Mom's leaving the house for any length of time; I would remain completely unrelaxed and in many cases inconsolable until her return.

I did not understand about the process of death and mourning back then. In a way, I thought it was neat during her Shiva, when a number of Jewish couples from all over the city stopped by one night and talked with her out on the balcony. I felt as though we were the star family of the Shul that week.

I was due to spend a third school year in Mrs. Wilkinson's class until modifications in the Special Education Program took precedence. First, Mrs. Wilkinson was moved to a managerial position. Next, Mr. Brinkman decided that there was a place for me in his classroom.

Starting from a few years back, Ray had been going to Beth Abraham nearly every Sunday afternoon from some point in October until May to rehearse with a choir which was becoming more and more famous. This choir was the

Beth Abraham Youth Chorale, which Moshe and I were to join later. Every year, they performed their annual concert at some point in May. During the summer immediately prior to my one and only school year in Mr. Brinkman's class, Ray toured Israel and England with the choir. Moshe and I could not help being somewhat jealous of him. Both of us felt that over the latter half of the preceding school year and on into that summer, Ray boasted too much about going on tour. He went for four weeks and had a very good time. He returned with candy and souvenirs for all of us.

***

During the last three years that I was in special education classes for the visually impaired (1975–76, 1976–77, and 1977–78), Mom worked in the deaf–blind classroom of Grant School.

Sometimes I would walk down to her classroom after my class let out and ride home with her when she was ready. At other times, Moshe and I had to take the bus home. Once Moshe had transferred to Hillel Academy, of course I rode to and home from school by myself. It did not make much difference to me that Mom was working in the same building that I was attending school in, except that she would occasionally sneak in an occasional "Hi" when she saw me in the hallway. However, there was one occurrence at this time where our joint attendance in the same school did pose a problem for me.

At the start of my second year in Mrs. Wilkinson's

class, I was enrolled in a Sunday school class at Beth Abraham. The Sunday school teacher was to be none other than Mom herself. I was scarcely going on eight at the time, and I thought it was very special to have my mother be the class teacher. However, when class began, I could not seem to make a distinction in my mind between her being Mom and being the teacher. To make a long story short, I continuously stole her attention from the rest of the class for two Sundays.

Just after class on the second Sunday, Mom complained to Dad about my actions in class. Dad told me that I had to look at her more as a teacher than a mother while I was in class. I did not understand what he meant and did not think I was doing anything wrong. Just before class the third Sunday, Mom detailed to Dad the particular events of the previous week that had bothered her the most. He became infuriated when he found out that I had acted worse than he had originally thought. He thereupon punished me, forcing me to stay in my bedroom during the entire time of Sunday school. I still could not understand what the problem was, and did not understand why I was being punished.

The following week, I was switched to a Sunday school class at Beth Jacob, a class taught by JoAnn Basch. She was delighted to have me as a student, although her friendship with me outside of class got in the way a couple of times during my two years in her Sunday school class. When she was forced to discipline me, she threatened to tell my parents about my bad behavior, but she never did. This kept our friendship intact and caused me to respect her even more as a dignified person.

Chapter 8

David Tishbaum and the Start of My Jewish Learning

It was during this time in my life that I received most of my Jewish learning. This would not have happened had it not been for David Tishbaum. David was a very kindhearted man who loved all Jews. He had never been able to settle down and get married and did not have steady work at that time. He insisted on teaching every single Jew Torah, according to each person's special learning abilities. It did not matter whether a person was religious, ignorant, unbelieving, young, or old. He would find every way possible to get through to anybody at any age in order to teach Torah. He was never afraid of getting into an argument about how religion should be practiced.

My instruction with him began when I was seven years old. David had been coming over to our house in order to teach my older brothers Torah, and I wondered when it would be my turn. Finally, he walked in one evening and insisted on studying especially with me. He began to teach me the words of the Shema and Shemoneh Esrei. At other times, he would telephone our house and study with me over the phone; some of those sessions lasted 45 minutes or even longer. When he was not teaching me how to pray, he was telling me Bible stories from Genesis and Exodus. No matter what time of day or night David was teaching me, he would drill and drill until I had committed to memory what he was teaching me, to the point that I could recite it back to him exactly as I was supposed to. When my mind would wander, he would tease me, but he stopped the lesson when he realized that I had had all I could take.

David Tishbaum had a very loving quality. It was hard to say no to him. At times, Dad was not in the mood to go to Shul for services. When David called, however, Dad usually agreed to go. Even when Dad said no, David would plead with him until he got his wish. Eventually, members of Shomrei Emuna began to grow weary of David's intensity and wished he would leave people alone. However, everybody felt that David was doing something good for them that nobody else could.

***

When I was about nine, Mom enrolled me in the Community Hebrew School. The primer which they were to use was ordered for me from the Jewish Braille

Institute. At the time, classes there were being taught by Rabbi Fox's wife. Her personality in the classroom differed from what I remembered from Junior Congregation in Beth Jacob. By that time, I had grown accustomed to learning at school as largely being preceded by fun and games. Although Mrs. Wilkinson had had me copy a lot of sentences and solve a lot of math problems, her lectures were either easy to follow or laden with humor, which made them easier to follow. I had never felt any extreme expectation to be especially studious in the classroom.

Following what I would later understand was the correct procedure, Mrs. Fox was teaching our Hebrew School class the same way that any good teacher should teach a class. That is, she demanded a great amount of attention and studiousness from her students. Not understanding that this was how normal school at that time was taught, I felt her patience to be thin, and she thought I was not trying my hardest. I gave up after only two classes.

Concerned, Mom spoke to David Tishbaum over the phone, asking him for some help. I did not realize this, but he and Dad had sat down and figured out the Hebrew Braille code together. (Dad had forgotten it by that time.) Either David or Dad got hold of the print copy of the primer which the class in Hebrew School was using, and David himself worked one-on-one with me for several weeks on Shabbos afternoon until I learned how to read Hebrew Braille.

I'll never forget my first session with David in learning how to read Hebrew. I had been waiting up for him very late one Saturday night in the middle of the winter. Mom made donuts for us, using a donut maker that I had been given as a present on my last birthday. Finally, it was ten o'clock, and I was very tired. David walked into the house after I was already in bed. Dad came into my bedroom and told me that David wanted to do just a little bit of learning that night. I got a bathrobe on over my pajamas and put slippers on my feet. I walked into the dining room, where David already had my Braille primer open. I began to read what little I remembered from Hebrew school. Then I read my first word, "Abba," and David became very excited. He began to sing a traditional song of congratulations very loudly, then had me say the correct blessing and eat part of a donut, which I had next to no appetite for. He let me go back to bed after that.

This was not the only time I had to leave my bed to learn with David that late in the night. For some reason, Dad always insisted that I get out of bed and learn with David no matter how late he finally arrived at our home. Thinking back on it, it was probably just as well that I did this, as otherwise, I might not have had the chance to learn. When I could finally read Hebrew Braille, David had me bring Moshe's Siddur and Chumash to him so that he could further teach me. On the side, he also taught me laws of festivals and other institutions of religious Judaism. When he taught me Chumash, he would do more drilling on the English meaning of words than when he taught me prayer. Consequently, I grew to recite prayers daily, not understanding most of what I was saying. However, if it had not been for David, I probably would not know nearly as much about Jewish life and keeping Halacha as I do.

Chapter 9

School, 1977–78

Ray's Bar Mitzvah

That school year, 1977–78, my only one in Mr. Brinkman's class, was probably the most interesting school year of my life. Mr. Brinkman was a fantastic teacher who maintained an individualized relationship with each and every one of his students. At the cost of a great deal of time, he tried to make learning as interesting as he could. Among many other things, he enjoyed taking us on field trips. One that I remember best was to the art museum. There was a "Skin Show" there, which featured many containers of liquids surrounded by skin coverings. All of us in the class stayed on our best behavior on field trips so that he would take us on more of them. That school year was also very interesting and eventful outside of Mr. Brinkman's classroom.

That school year, Moshe entered the Beth Abraham Youth Chorale. They commissioned and performed a work known as "The Day of Rest." The work was based on the

Sabbath liturgy. Moshe walked around the house singing his second soprano part. This greatly annoyed Ray, who quit choir in the middle of the year.

Ray's Bar Mitzvah occurred on Thanksgiving of that school year. For two months before, Dad and Mom had become increasingly busy preparing for the affair. They bought a lot of food wholesale in order to put on a huge Thanksgiving dinner at Hillel Academy for nearly the entire Jewish community.

Meanwhile, the week after I turned nine, Charlie got his driver's license. That was on Ray's birthday: November 4, 1977. Two days later, Dad and Mom decided to let Charlie practice his driving and take Moshe and Ray to choir rehearsal at Beth Abraham. Charlie, Ray, and Moshe left the house as I sat down to lunch at the kitchen table.

Minutes later, Charlie bounded back into the house, announcing that he had just had a serious accident. The rest of us walked out of the house up Cory Drive to the site of the accident, where we found our station wagon, which Dad and Mom had owned for four years, smashed beyond repair. Ray had stayed behind from the choir rehearsal to act as a witness.

Apparently, Charlie had somehow crashed into a disabled car which belonged to a sick woman who lived on that street. When Charlie hit the car with the station wagon, he forced the car—which, according to the woman, had not been in operation for at least a year and a half—to jut out onto the sidewalk. When the police investigation was complete, Mom took me over to feel the damage. At that time, I was learning the different meanings of the words "major" and "minor." I had heard that there were both "major" and "minor" car accidents. I asked, "Is this major?" Ray said, "Yes, Chaim, this is very, very major."

I was terror-stricken, wondering how Mom and I would get to school and back after this, given that we rode together. The nice woman whose car Charlie hit kept reassuring me that if Mom had to go to the same school that I did because she had to work there, she would make sure that I would get there also. I had no way of knowing this at the time, but that woman was taken to a hospital moments after we Segals left the scene and went home.

Two weeks later, as there were still many, many errands to be taken care of in preparation for the Bar Mitzvah, Mom bought a car, a Malibu, from another staff member at school for $75. It was to tide us over until the Bar Mitzvah. After that, she and Dad would have to look for a brand-new car.

Close to Thanksgiving, Mom began to skip days of work. Amid the chaos, Dad often drove me to school late on some of those mornings. On a few of these trips, I had the opportunity to see how food was sold wholesale. Dad stopped at warehouses where he and service people put huge boxes with big cans and containers of food into the back sections of the car. On some afternoons, Mom took me out of school early to shop for a suit for the occasion. She insisted that all of us wear brand-new suits to the Bar Mitzvah service.

The day of the Bar Mitzvah, there was a splendid affair, but it was boring for Moshe and me at times. The entire Goldman family came down from Milwaukee. Of course

Uncle Bobby came down from Cleveland, accompanied by a distant cousin named Albert. There was something strange about Albert. He had a weird accent, and much of what he said did not seem to make sense. However, I could tell that he really liked and enjoyed our company. Being still quite immature for my age, I didn't like it that Mom was at Hillel Academy for nearly the entire night before the affair, and then there the majority of the day of the affair, cooking and cleaning.

Dad spent most of his time talking to Adolph Goldman when he was not helping out at Hillel Academy. When I woke up that Thanksgiving morning, I was very excited about going to the Bar Mitzvah. However, I was disappointed that Mom was not in the house. My disappointment was magnified when I realized that nobody in the house who was around and unoccupied seemed to know where my suit was. As I walked into the front of the house to ask Dad for help, I found him fully engaged in conversation with Adolph. Looking up from his conversation and seeing me still in my pajamas, he said, "Go get dressed, Hyim; we have to leave soon."

I responded, "But I need my suit," as he resumed talking to Adolph, as if my suit was supposed to magically appear from nowhere. I went and did my morning necessities and came back, to try asking Dad for my suit once again. Upon seeing me, he once again stated, "Go get dressed, Hyim," and resumed conversing with Adolph, without paying any heed to my needing his help. I realized that I had to do something daring in order to get his attention, so that hopefully he would listen to me.

A few times before, when I had felt that Dad was being unfair, I had put plastic food wrap bags over my head, after Ray had told me that you could cause yourself to suffocate and die by doing this. I figured that if Dad saw me suffocating, that would be sure to stop his conversation and allow me to tell him that I needed my suit if he wanted me to get dressed. I walked into the kitchen, took a plastic bag from where they were kept, and put it on my head. I walked back into the dining room where Dad and Adolph were still talking and began to boldly walk back and forth in an area where I would not be missed.

Next thing I knew, I heard somebody jump up from the table. A fraction of a second later, Dad grabbed me around the neck. He threw the plastic bag off my head, taking my yarmulke with it, and began to yell at me as Adolph walked out of the room. Dad bent me over and began to give me the hardest spanking of my life, which must have gone on for nearly a minute. He insisted that I was baiting him, and that this was just a silly thing that I had done to get attention. He threatened that if he ever saw me do this again, the punishment would be far more serious. Finally, as he concluded the spanking, he shrieked, "Why do you do these things that bug the hell out of me?"

I choked out through my sobbing, "I need my suit!"

At that point, he finally realized his wrongdoing, but he was still annoyed at my having put an end to his conversation with Adolph.

He snapped, "Okay, come on! I'll get you the suit!"

He then angrily searched through the closet in the bedroom that Moshe and I shared, but he did not find the suit. He instructed me to come into his bedroom, where he found the suit in his closet. He told me to sit down on his bed, gave me the suit and a white shirt to go with it, slapped me in the face, then left his bedroom with a slam of the door.

A concerned member of the Goldman family came into the bedroom and talked with me, trying to comfort me, as I had begun crying once again. Dad came and ordered whoever it was out, then hit me once again. I cried for about another minute as Dad left, and the person came back again, reassuring me that everything would be okay. I remember vowing to kill Dad later that day. Whoever it was who had been coming into the room told me to relax.

I rode over to the Bar Mitzvah feeling sullen. Ray had wanted me to have a small part in the service. Not knowing much of the liturgy that was acceptable for a minor to lead during a Bar Mitzvah, the only thing which he thought I could do was open the Ark, as the Torah would be read that morning. Someone made a mistake, and the wrong person was called to open the Ark. I got to close the Ark, but somehow did not feel satisfied with the service.

While many congregants stood and prayed, I was trying to put together a plan of how to kill Dad. Eventually, I gave up on this, but I began to miss Mom. I wanted very badly to tell her about what had happened. At a certain point in the service, one of the Goldman brothers took me on a walk through the building. I had heard from somebody that Mom was in the kitchen of the building. I asked the person with me to take me to the kitchen, and he did. But as soon as we opened the door and said "Hi," Mom angrily shouted, "Hey! Get him out of the kitchen! We're all trying to do some work around here!" This made me feel even worse, but by this point, I was beyond tears. I simply could not understand why the important people had to be so busy just to get this thing going.

In my walk through the building, I missed the candy being handed out to be thrown at Ray. I was seated in a chair just as David Tishbaum was beginning a speech. He spoke about how Ray was a very good Jew, including the fact that he made a Beracha over everything that he put in his mouth. I was disappointed at not having candy to throw at Ray at the conclusion of David's speech.

At the conclusion of the service, there was a mix–up of some sort and we did not have refreshments as Mom had planned. When I complained that I wanted some candy, one of the Goldman brothers hunted around and found a huge bag of Hershey bars, which he gave me. To my relief, Dad, whose mood had somehow switched to a jolly one which stayed with him for the rest of the day, allowed me to take the bag of Hershey bars back home with us.

That afternoon, Moshe and I found it hard to stay out of our bedroom, which had been given to members of the Goldman family to sleep off their previous night's Greyhound bus ride. Getting bored with one toy or game which we had taken from the bedroom, we would go back in and get another one, waking Sarah, the sister, who claimed not to mind. Charlie felt that what we were doing was unfair. He suddenly gathered the two of us together and said we were going for a walk. Despite damp November cold, he took us to the playground of a nearby park and made sure we worked off some of our restlessness before returning home with us. Then, a couple from Columbus who were good friends of ours at the time stopped by, and there was a long game of skittles; we brothers, the Goldman boys, and the husband played.

Finally, it was time to go back over to Hillel Academy for Thanksgiving dinner. On our arrival, JoAnn Basch was playing Jewish music on the piano in the school's multi-purpose room. After a Minchah in the library, guests from far and wide in the community joined us for the big Thanksgiving dinner. There were speeches and much food, but too much seriousness led to mischief. Shortly before Bensching, Uncle Bobby and Charlie had a pie fight on the stage with an apple pie. Even at my young age, I did not think this was very funny. Ray never forgot the incident. When he got married 14 years later, he insisted that no pies whatsoever be brought to the reception.

Chapter 10

Wild Winter Weather

After Ray's Bar Mitzvah, things began to quiet down at home for a while. Dad's anxiety mounted again, however, as he and Mom began the search for a new car. Meanwhile, we were trying to endure the most grueling winter that I can remember.

That winter featured the notorious Blizzard of 1978, which occurred on Thursday, January 26th. Prior to the blizzard, we had had several massive snowstorms, which usually resulted in our being off school the next day. At one point, we had an entire foot of snow on the ground, which kept us out of school for about four days straight.

There was a block of time before the blizzard that we were in school. If I remember correctly, the temperature outside was rather warm the day before the blizzard. I remember lying on Mom's bed the night before, listening to a moderate rain falling outside, suspecting that we would not have school the next day, even though the temperature outside was not cold enough for snow.

I woke up a little after five o'clock the next morning to the sound of the wind against the house. I had heard the term "blizzard" before and somehow knew that this must be one. I begged Mom, who was lying awake in bed next to me, to allow me to put on some clothing and to go out with me, so that I could experience the blizzard in full force. She cautioned me that we could not move away from the edge of our property, as people were getting lost a mere four feet from their cars.

She and I put some clothes on and walked outside the front door. It seemed as though the entire world had become made up of nothing but cold and snow. Later that day, Mom, Ray, Moshe, and I went outside to try to shovel snow off the driveway. Mom knew this would be to no avail, but she wanted to show Moshe and me how this blizzard differed from a normal snowfall. As I tried to shovel, my cheeks hurt from the stinging cold, and the wind was undoing in seconds what it should have taken us 20 minutes to complete. We were outside for less than five minutes.

The blizzard ended sometime after I went to bed that night. School did not open again until later the following week. Having no place to go, I was bored out of my mind during this time off from school. It felt good to return to Mr. Brinkman's classroom when school reopened.

About a month after the blizzard, Mom and Dad bought their new car, a blue station wagon which ran on unleaded gasoline. This car had two "way–back" seats, which we used while Moshe and I were still young. This car reminded me of the one that Mrs. Estice, our former driver, had used to transport us to and from school four years before. The car was to last us for about five years before Dad and Mom decided to get rid of it.

Chapter 11

Singing, New School Prospects, and a New Dog

In April of that year, at Beth Abraham, Dad, Mom, and I attended the Saturday evening Bar Mitzvah of a person whom Charlie had helped to train. That evening, Cantor Kopmar, Cantor of Beth Abraham Synagogue and director of the Beth Abraham Youth Chorale, sought me out and invited me to join in the fall.

That school year ended on a happy note. I was told that from then on, for the rest of my schooling, I would be attending regular classes with sighted students. I thought this would be very challenging and wondered what it would feel like.

To add to the excitement, we found ourselves with a new puppy.

A woman who worked with Mom in the deaf–blind classroom and who had formerly been an aide in Mrs. B.'s classroom was out with her husband at a parade when they discovered two abandoned puppies, a male and a female.

She and her husband took the male puppy for themselves, and we took the female, naming her Tippy. Tippy was a black dog with white–tipped paws. Although she seemed very intelligent as she grew out of puppyhood, she tended to run after things and people, trying to bite them from behind. She bit some people up the street and made friends with others. Any one of us who would accidentally awaken her would be sure to have a set of fangs close around a hand or foot. Within the year and three months which followed, she bit three people, which required that we have her put to sleep. Although we knew it was the right decision, we felt sad to lose her. We had her through my third grade year and had her put to sleep just after Moshe's Bar Mitzvah.

Meanwhile, the summer following my year in Mr. Brinkman's class was somewhat uneventful. Rami Ranan came to visit at a certain point, and Moshe had to have an operation at the nearby Good Samaritan Hospital.

The week following Moshe's operation, Beth Jacob moved into a brand–new building on North Main Street. It had been constructed over the course of the past year.

Now our family had no choice but to begin attending Shomrei Emuna on a regular basis.

Chapter 12

Rabbi Rottenberg

At that time, the only thing I minded at Shomrei Emuna was the rabbi's singing. Rabbi Rottenberg of blessed memory, our rabbi at the time, was a Chasid who was born in Poland; his father had been the rabbi of a community. He displayed much fervor when he sang and spoke, and especially his singing was extremely loud. At Shaloshudos, which he instituted, he led the congregation in appropriate song, followed by his last speech of Shabbos. One song in particular, Benei Haycholo, had a very haunting melody. For a few years, whenever he sang this particular Chasidic song in his loud voice, I feared that I was soon to be kidnapped. Eventually, like everything else concerning him, I got used to the song.

One element of Rabbi Rottenberg's voice had a sound that I thought resembled oil. Thus I believed for a long time that he literally ran on oil. I figured that in secrecy, somebody poured oil through a hole somewhere on his body, and that that was what gave him his abundant energy. His intensity scared me, but face-to-face with him, I found him to be a gentle, kindhearted man. As I began to attend Shomrei Emuna on a regular basis, I began to grow accustomed to Rabbi Rottenberg's loud, shrill singing and intense speeches. However, I understood very little of what he said in the speeches. When he left the community during the summer of 1979, I actually felt a void during the first Shaloshudos of his absence, and I left the basement crying.

Chapter 13

Collecting Some Real-World Experience

Meanwhile, my third-grade year, the school year of 1978–79, offered some unique positive and negative experiences. The school year itself got off to a late start. That was because the vast majority of teachers in the Dayton City Public School system held the longest teachers' strike in the history of the school system. The strike lasted through the entire month of September. The teachers in question had threatened to hold the strike until November, until school board officials promised a pay increase.

One day in early September, Mom and I went to Grant School, where I managed to borrow two elementary Braille books from the school's Braille library for my reading pleasure and practice. Those were the first long stories I read from beginning to end by myself; at the time, that was a major accomplishment.

On another September day that year, I received my first collect call, which resulted in a much–needed learning experience. It happened one afternoon when Mom was out, leaving me all alone in the house. Moshe had a doctor's appointment that day, to measure the process of his recuperation from the operation. This appointment would determine whether or not he could go swimming again. Naturally, Moshe had been anxious about this appointment from the time he had awakened that morning. On the bus back from Hillel Academy, it was hard for him to contain his restlessness.

At this time, Ray and Moshe rode the school bus together to and from Hillel Academy. When Moshe began to act in a way that Ray felt was inappropriate, Ray would have the driver come to a stop, excuse himself and Moshe, and force Moshe to leave the bus. If they were within walking distance of home, Ray would force Moshe to walk the rest of the way home with him. If they were still a good distance away, he would call Mom or somebody else for a ride.

Naturally, Moshe was anxious to make the appointment that day on time. On the bus, he began to display behavior which upset Ray. Ray interpreted this as a "tantrum" and removed himself and Moshe from the bus. The bus was closer to Hillel Academy than home. Ray thought it best to try to call Mom for a ride, unless the RTA bus would arrive soon.

I did not learn about many practical aspects of everyday life, things that were common knowledge, until later in life than most people. At this time, I was about a month and a half shy of my tenth birthday. I had heard the term "collect call," but I thought it was a call that was made so that someone would literally be collected from a house or building—or if not a person, then certainly a large amount of money or many assets. I imagined that if I received a collect call and agreed to it, they would send someone or possibly even a band of angry men out to storm into the house and snatch me and/or everything in the house away for good. If I disagreed, collection would happen faster and would be even more brutal.

That day, it just so happened that Ray had very little money on him and decided to try to call home collect.

I was eating a snack in the kitchen when the phone rang. I picked up the receiver and said "Hello?" as I normally did. A woman on the other end said, "This is a collect call from Ray Segal. Do you accept the charges?"

I was dumbfounded and frightened. I said no on the spot and promptly hung up the receiver, fearing that maybe having said no might cause me to be collected faster. As I resumed my snack, the phone rang again. I picked up the receiver and said, "Hello?" The same woman said the exact same thing as before. This time, I gave her a few seconds of silence as a thought dawned on me. Maybe this "collect" business meant that Ray was either trying to take something from Dad and Mom or give them something. However, I did not hear Ray's voice, only his name. I could not be sure. I said, "I'm sorry. You would have to speak to my parents about that and they are not home now. They are in charge of the money around here. All I get is allowance." I thereupon hung up the phone, even more scared than before.

Seconds after I hung up, the phone rang for a third time. I had half a mind not to answer, but I thought that if I was to be collected, it was probably on a command from God and thus meant to be. I picked up the receiver and did not even have a chance to say a word. For a third time, this operator said, "A collect call from Ray Segal—do you accept the charges?" She tried to enunciate every syllable to be sure I understood. Then, to my relief, I heard Ray call out, "Chaim, say yes!" Although Ray sounded angry, I felt more comfortable dealing with this woman hearing that he was actually on the line. I said yes, and the operator hung up.

Ray then angrily explained to me how collect calls work. He explained how he had forced Moshe off the bus after Moshe had thrown a tantrum. He apologized for being so upset with me. Moshe missed his appointment that day, due to how late it got when Ray and he ended up taking an RTA bus home.

***

I joined the Beth Abraham Youth Chorale that fall. At my tryout, Cantor Kopmar played some notes on the piano and had me hum and sing familiar tunes for him. Upon hearing my voice, he decided he could not pass me up, but he warned me that I had to be serious and pay close attention in rehearsals. I would be singing first soprano. That year, the choir commissioned and performed a work

The Sayzeh Song — Book One

known as "Proverbs of the Sages," composed by Morton Gold. The work consisted of the words of Mishnah, which were sayings by ancient prominent sages on how to live a moral life.

***

I would venture to say that this school year was my worst one at Grant School. Busing was in full swing in the Dayton City school system. Never having been mainstreamed before, I had no way of knowing exactly what to expect. I could hardly believe it when, on my first day of third grade, I was seated in a classroom with nearly 45 other students. The students had a great mixture of regional dialects among them. For the most part, I assumed that we all lived the same when we went home— except for the fact that I was the only one who came from a family of religious Jews who kept kosher, Shabbos, and Yomtiv. However, many of the students acted in a manner which I could not understand.

Our teacher, Mrs. McDowell, had a terrible time controlling the majority of the students in the class. She was a nice, caring woman, but not in good health. In fact, during February of that school year, she left for an extended amount of time, which lasted clear into April. Ms. Hamilton, the woman who was called upon to substitute for her, knew Mom and me from the special education unit of the school. Although she had worked with various levels of mental retardation, it was no easier for her to control the class than anybody else.

Students talked while teachers were addressing the class, purposely distracted the teachers while they were trying to teach concepts and course work, ate candy during lessons, threw things at each other across the classroom, and did many other things which distressed those of us who were trying to learn something or make going to school a positive experience. With both teachers, the sound of a student being paddled out in the hallway was one that I had to bear more than once a day. Although I knew that the students deserved it, I considered it unfair that the rest of us had to hear the sound. I wondered why it was so hard for these children to behave themselves, the way I did.

There were some good things that happened that year, both inside and outside of school. Soon after the start of school, I developed a friendship with a classmate of mine named Teresa Hargess. When she would see me looking sad, she would do anything in her power to cheer me up. She went to church regularly and was highly respectful of my being religious. In addition, I went to the second–grade classroom for reading class and made friends with a nice girl there named Laura.

That year, Dad and Mom gave me a splendid birthday party. My actual birthday fell on the same Sunday that choir rehearsals were to start. The night before, Teresa Hargess and a few other acquaintances came over for games and Halloween donuts. Then Dad and Mom took us out for a hay ride and Halloween celebration at a farm a short distance from the city.

That year, I completed most of my written class and

homework assignments in Braille. Ms. Hild, an itinerant teacher, worked privately with me three times a week. She improved my typing skills, taught me how to use a slate and stylus, attempted to teach me how to sign my name, and transcribed my written class and homework assignments from Braille to print.

In addition, my mobility lessons became more intense. Previously, various mobility instructors had had me walk around, trying to visually follow the line between the blacktop and sidewalk outside the school. They had also had me find balls with what little vision I possessed, and they had allowed me to jump on a trampoline and ride an exercise bicycle in a special room at school in order to boost my gross motor skills.

That year, Mr. Craig Alan, the mobility instructor, tried to make me work extra hard at finding balls and other things using both vision and sound. I purposely did not cooperate with him, because I felt it unnecessary to be doing this. He reprimanded me time and time again and made sure I followed his directions despite my attitude. Two years later, he admitted to me that he had been having some personal difficulties that year, difficulties which had made him more short-tempered than he had realized.

Chapter 14

Music and Moving

Over Thanksgiving vacation of that year, the Goldmans came in from Milwaukee once again, bringing a brand–new stereo with them as a present for Mom. Ray helped the Goldman brothers set it up, then tried to keep Moshe and me away from it for fear we would break it; he was only successful for about two or three weeks. However, Ray had absolutely nothing to fear, as this stereo lasted well into the period of our story ahead. It had a very powerful sound, and Moshe and I were glad to have it in the house. Its features included an AM/FM radio, a turntable, and an eight–track recorder and player.

About three weeks following Thanksgiving weekend, we Segals began to accelerate the process of moving seven houses down the block, into our very own home. We had actually begun the process in mid–October by moving some items of lesser importance that we could temporarily live without. Our decision to move out of the duplex was due to us boys growing older. Very often, especially on Shabbos, we made a lot of noise without meaning to. This disturbed the Wills family downstairs. The mother of the family would either call and let our phone ring a few times or ring our doorbell to give us a signal to be quiet.

Our first night in the new house was the night of Wednesday, December 20, 1978. However, the majority of our move took place during winter vacation the following week. I'd had no idea how time–consuming the move would be, nor how greatly Dad's mood would be affected by it. All of us had to work extra hard for about four days, hauling our belongings down the street.

A detailed description of the house will follow in the first chapter of Book Two of my story. Dad and Mom would stay in this house for the rest of Dad's life.

About two months after our move, I switched piano teachers. JoAnn Basch had a number of difficulties and could not always give Moshe and me her undivided attention during our piano lessons. She was reluctant to give us up as students, and Mom did not tell her she was finding another teacher for us. The teacher Mom found was probably one of the best pianists in the city. Unfortunately, he felt that there was a particular way that the piano should be played and that nothing except perfection would do. To make a long story short, I only lasted a few months with this teacher. Later on, I went back to JoAnn Basch for lessons on and off, when our schedules permitted it. I didn't really need to study with someone other than her. Most piano playing in my life has been for fun and strictly by ear. I also enjoy playing electronic synthesizer keyboards.

At some point during the second half of that same school year, Charlie purchased his own stereo system with money earned from a sandblasting job in a local factory. His system was quite different from Mom's, or the one that Moshe was to purchase the fall following his Bar Mitzvah. It had separate components rather than being one unit. Charlie had wanted to be sure that his system had excellent quality sound, and it did. Dad could not understand why he was spending so much money on a stereo system and went through a period of nonstop grief on account of Charlie's purchase. I could not understand why Dad was so upset about this matter. After all, Charlie was earning and spending his own money on the system. Once Charlie's high-quality stereo system was set up, I heard great varieties of music coming out of his bedroom in the years that followed.

My third-grade year did not end on an especially happy note. Although I was glad to be getting away from that class, I began to feel that something was missing from my life. I could not define it, but felt it had something to do with not having as much activity outside the house as it appeared that other children my age did.

That summer, there were many days when Moshe and I went to the Jewish Community Center. We swam until we were tired of the pool, went and got food at the concession stand, then resumed swimming for a long while. Mom, Ray, and the two of us took a trip to Milwaukee that summer, stopping in Chicago for a kosher meal on our way up.

Chapter 15

Seeds of Misunderstanding

That same summer following Rabbi Rottenberg's leaving, members of Shomrei Emuna decided to try to have what was known as a SEED Program. The word SEED was an acronym for Summer Educational Experience Development. A SEED Program consisted of five or six post–high school Yeshiva students with one or two married couples; the husband in one of the couples was a rabbi. In our case, the Yeshiva students were from the two branches of Telshea Yeshiva near Cleveland and in Chicago.

When the prospect was introduced, a few congregants, especially the current president, were extremely doubtful that our small Shul could deliver on what was needed to run it. Even as late as the night before the arrival of the students, there was a great deal of tension in the air. Somehow, truly with God's help, the SEED Program was successfully launched and was a tremendous success. Other SEED Programs followed for the next three consecutive summers, then during summers here and there throughout the remainder of Shomrei Emuna's existence.

Upon hearing that Shomrei Emuna was going to have a SEED Program, I took that literally and figured that some or all members of Shomrei Emuna were going to plant some type of seeds in the Shul's back yard or at some local garden site. Were we going to plant fruit trees, or maybe regular trees? Who knew? When I heard talk at Shul and around the house concerning the "SEED boys from Telshea," I figured that these "boys" were coming to learn Torah with some of us at coincidentally the same time that we would be planting seeds. I was more excited about the planting of seeds than I was about learning Torah with these Yeshiva boys from Telshea. After all, by that point, Charlie had begun speaking so negatively concerning his experience at Telshea that I wondered what good all this could amount to.

Needless to say, I was dismayed when the Yeshiva Bachurim arrived during the first week of the Three Weeks and began to run both individual and group learning— with no mention of planting seeds. Moshe and I went to Shomrei Emuna in the mornings to learn, as that was the time of day set aside for young people to learn with the Bachurim. The following week, despite the Nine Days, Moshe and I attended a water-oriented city camp, which handicapped our mornings. Although the evenings were set aside for adult learning, a few of the Bachurim were willing to learn with us in the evenings for that week instead. While we were at the water camp, Moshe would periodically say to me that he wished we were learning with the Bachurim. Personally, I preferred being at the water camp. Although I knew that learning Torah was important, I didn't think that my life depended on it.

During the last two weeks of the SEED Program, when Moshe and I resumed learning in the morning, an increasing number of people came in from the outside. The Bachurim who had been learning with me had begun to learn with other people instead. One morning, I sat in the Shul doing absolutely nothing as the entire time passed. A day or two later, I arrived and began to sit by myself once again. Fearing that a repeat of the previous experience was underway, I finally stood up crying. I began to make my way into the Shul's kitchen and over to the telephone to call Dad or Mom to pick me up.

It was lucky for me that David Tishbaum happened to be present, doing what he felt he could to oversee the program in his own way. Catching sight of me crying and upset, he comforted me and asked me what was wrong. When I told him that it looked as though I had come for nothing, he took it upon himself to learn with me. For every morning that followed until the end of the SEED Program, he either found someone to learn with me or did so himself.

Meanwhile, over the entire course of the SEED Program, I kept asking Mom every few days, "Where are the seeds?" Her persistent response was, "They're in the Shul." I kept patiently waiting until the day we would plant the seeds, and was dismayed when the SEED Program came to an end without anything happening in this regard.

The SEED Program ended the same morning that

Mom, Ray, Moshe, and I left for Milwaukee. Shortly after we crossed the Indiana border, I asked Mom a final time, "Where are the seeds for the SEED Program now?"

Assuming I understood by that point that the "seeds" in question were seeds of learning, she answered, "They went back."

Perplexed, I asked, "They went back? Where did they go back to? You kept telling me that the seeds were in the Shul! They weren't even planted!"

Finally realizing my gross misconception, Mom said, "Sure they were planted! These were seeds of learning!"

Feeling like a fool, I sadly said, "Oh, I thought we were going to actually plant seeds."

Moshe flatly stated, "I don't know what purpose that would have served."

I sat pondering what had just happened. I realized that these Telshea Bachurim were probably supposed to open the community up to the concept of learning more Torah. But if this was only for the summer, then why bother?

A year or two later, when I found out that these Yeshiva Bachurim were sacrificing a great portion of their short summer vacations to do this, I could not figure out why any of them would want to do such a thing. It would take over 30 years for me to finally understand.

Chapter 16

Moshe's Bar Mitzvah

My Fourth-Grade Year

Prior to our trip, during the Three Weeks, the record of "Proverbs of the Sages" arrived at our house. The day after Tisha B'Av, we all listened to it and enjoyed it very much. Then excitement pertaining to Moshe's upcoming Bar Mitzvah began to take hold.

School got off to a fairly good start that September. I was in fourth grade, and my teacher was Mrs. Baker. With the start of school came a series of rainstorms in connection with a notorious hurricane dubbed Hurricane Frederic. It occurred in August and September of 1979.

Moshe's Bar Mitzvah was held at Shomrei Emuna on Shabbos Morning, September 8, 1979. Again, Mom was involved with much preparation. However, as Moshe's Bar Mitzvah was considerably more modest than Ray's, less preparation was needed. For his Bar Mitzvah, Moshe led Congregation Shomrei Emuna for both the Shacharis and Musaf Services and chanted that week's Haftara. Given that we were blind, it was impossible for Moshe and me to read directly from the Torah scroll as most boys do on their Bar Mitzvahs. When services concluded, we all made our way to the Shul's kitchen for Kiddush, then proceeded to the basement for lunch.

At midnight that night, I sang with the Beth Abraham Youth Chorale, helping Cantor Kopmar to lead the Selichot service. This was the first time I had ever stayed up late for this service. Seeing that I was tired from the day's activities, Cantor Kopmar gave me the option of leaving the Bimah. I stuck it out, but missed Sunday school next morning.

Amid the excitement of Moshe's Bar Mitzvah, Mom decided that I should try to maintain a social life within the Jewish community that year. She had previously enrolled me in Beth Abraham's fourth-grade Sunday school class. When it turned out that there was not a teacher for that class, Mom was hired for the job. Not wanting to be in the same class that she was teaching, I opted to join their fifth-grade class instead. The teacher was a young Beth Abraham woman who seemed to take great pride in teaching. I already knew just about everything that she taught the class and what was in their textbooks, but I decided not to show off about it. However, at times I felt that I was wasting my time attending Beth Abraham's Sunday school when I learned with David Tishbaum on a fairly regular basis. Nevertheless, I did not regret attending; it helped to fill the day out, as it was followed by a choir rehearsal.

As a whole, my fourth–grade school year, 1979–1980, had a lot more to offer than my third–grade year, both inside and outside of school. That fall, I tried out for higher status in the Beth Abraham Youth Chorale and made it to Tour Choir in Training. Moshe was now fully in Tour Choir. He was also in the section of the choir with the best singers, the section known as Chamber Choir. I was a little envious of the prospect of him going all the way to California with the Tour Choir in March of that school year.

That year, we commissioned a work known as "Psalms of Abraham." It was called this for two reasons. First, the work had been composed especially for our choir, the Beth Abraham Youth Chorale. Second, the composer's name was Abraham Kaplan. The choir also performed versions of old, familiar Jewish songs; a modern arranger named Neil Levin had arranged some accompaniment to the songs for us.

Abraham Kaplan had a delightful sense of humor. I would not have had the chance to spend enough time with him to find this out if I hadn't been in Tour Choir in Training. One Sunday during March of that school year, CBS TV came to Beth Abraham and filmed the entire Tour Choir and Tour Choir in Training singing selections of the work "Psalms of Abraham." Before and during the filming, Abraham Kaplan himself took a hand at conducting us.

That October, I began to take private trumpet lessons in school. The teacher, Mr. Onger, played clarinet for the Dayton Philharmonic Orchestra. In years past, he had also backed the Beth Abraham Youth Chorale along with other Dayton Philharmonic musicians, and he recognized me from there. In order to teach me, Mr. Onger recorded the pieces and exercises from the beginner's trumpet book (and later on, band pieces) onto a cassette, and I learned them and played them for him. It took until mid–May to work through the book. Then he promoted me to the school's advanced band.

We spent our Thanksgiving vacation of that school year in Milwaukee with the Goldmans. We all had a very good time. However, Moshe and I were bored at certain moments of a museum visit, as we could not touch several of the displays.

I began to enjoy my mobility lessons more that year. Also, Mr. Alan worked with me using a special type of closed circuit TV, a CCTV video magnifier. (I remember it being referred to as visual tech.) It's a special camera device for the visually impaired; it has the form of a television set that enlarges print. Various controls on it also manage contrast and brightness. I began to be able to read more and more print letters and words with it. Mom and Dad had had one purchased for us a few years back, but we had not been using it much. To further motivate me, Mr. Alan gave me access to a computer Simon game. That spring, Dad bought Moshe and me one as a Pesach gift.

Chapter 17

Two Unsettling Incidents

It was in mid–February of that year that I learned how one word could be of tremendous danger and insult.

For about a month, a certain black girl in our class had been calling me "bald–headed." I did not have the slightest idea why until somebody outside of school pointed out that it could have been because I kept my head covered by a yarmulke, a skullcap. In past years, Moshe and I had had considerably fewer problems with wearing yarmulkes in Grant School. This is probably why I did not make the connection.

Mom and Dad had taught me not to say or think bad things about the black people among whom we lived. Up until this point, in my own mind, I had decided that they were people, just as we were, and it was okay for us to like some and fear others. It was not as if we necessarily liked every Jew in town.

However, many Jews we knew and with whom I hung around in my younger days talked negatively about blacks, using derogatory terms to describe them. Probably the term I heard most was "shvartza." There were other terms used to describe them that I did not know the meaning of. Until this point, I had assumed, after hearing the word spoken by other Jews, that the word "nigger" simply meant somebody who bothered you at any given point in time. I had no idea that this was a nasty term used by whites to refer to black people, and that it was used by blacks themselves to refer to each other.

Looking back on it, I would say that it's better that I learned my lesson on this matter in the way I did, rather than having had to suffer a lot more embarrassment later on.

The girl who had been calling me "bald-headed" was forced to sit next to me at the lunch table that day. While I was eating, she began to squeeze an orange onto my winter coat, causing it to be totally soiled and unwearable until I could get it laundered. In an effort to make her stop and leave me alone, I began to spell some cuss words out to her, words that regarded her. One of these words was "nigger." In addition to this, I made a second mistake which only made matters worse.

Starting a few years prior to that time, Dad had begun to boost my pride in a manner which I now feel was inexcusable. When he discovered that I had come to a valuable realization or a good point in understanding, he would call me a "smart-ass Jewish kid." Sometimes he did this in public places, such as the supermarket. I began to take him seriously, and I began to think that I was smarter than anybody else in Grant School except for Mr. Nilson (the principal), the teachers working under him, and certain other staff members. In addition, David Tishbaum had begun to have me think and believe that our having the Torah made us the best, most powerful nation on earth. I began to think that because we walked to Shul on Shabbos in sub-zero weather, and because we had eight-day-long holidays like Pesach, we Jews were smarter than any other people alive.

In my stupidity that February day in the lunch room, I stated to this girl that our religion was better than hers. I further stated that all her holidays were only one day long, whereas a few of our festivals went on for eight days. Her response to that was that she celebrated Christmas, and the only reason why we did not do so was because we were dumb. Then the two of us began to shower each other with personal insults for a few minutes. Finally, she called one of the staff people on duty over and explained, from her point of view, what had been going on and described my bad actions.

Ever since I had started attending mainstream classes, I had rarely had to be disciplined. This was about to change.

That day happened to be a Monday. The janitor and art teacher who had lunchroom duty decided to suspend me from the lunch table for the rest of the week. On Thursday evening of that week, I decided to begin writing a journal. It was based on one that Moshe was putting together for school in a large, loose-leaf notebook. The lunchroom incident was the first thing I wrote about in my journal. The following Monday, when I attempted to return to my class's lunch table, before I was admitted, the janitor asked me if I could behave myself. It was not until the middle of my time in junior high that I recognized what I had done as totally unacceptable.

***

A few weeks later, another incident worth mentioning happened. Moshe and I had gotten into a heated physical fight in our bedroom when I grabbed his yarmulke and refused to give it back. As I stood there boldly holding it, he began to strangle me. As I stood my ground, he choked me even harder, asking, "Are you going to give me my yarmulke?"

All of a sudden, I felt that I was rising upward into a cave of sorts. The two of us had been watching the sun setting outside the bedroom window. Now I felt as though I was coming closer to the sun. For a split second, I sensed the presence of an avalanche of boxes of Duncan Hines Double Fudge Brownie Mix—my favorite food at the time. Then I sensed the presence of my maternal grandfather. I heard Moshe's voice, sounding as if it was calling from somewhere far off. "Are you going to give me back my yarmulke?" I then heard Mom's father calling from above me. I sensed his presence from above, as though he was on a ship that was about to sail away.

"You'd better give it back to him already," he said. "It's

not time for you to be up here yet. You've got a long life ahead of you." He gave a pleasurable laugh, then vanished.

I cried out to Moshe, "Yes," and tried to feel for the top of his head, but my right hand was almost too numb to feel anything. I forget exactly what happened to his yarmulke, but I remember his letting go of my neck. No sooner did he let go than I felt as though I was slipping farther and farther away from the sun with each second. Then I felt as though I was re-entering the house and falling back into the bedroom, landing on my feet.

According to Moshe, I acted totally hysterical for a few minutes after the incident. He made me promise not to tell, as Mom and Dad had threatened punishment should he strangle me again. However, as frightened as I had been, I could not help telling them; I did so later that evening, while Moshe was at a choir rehearsal. His punishment was that he had to forfeit his stereo for a month.

Moshe went on tour to Los Angeles about a month after the lunchroom incident. Although I was jealous of him, I was glad to have the use of his stereo (which he had purchased the previous fall with his Bar Mitzvah money) all to myself. His stereo included an AM/FM radio, a turntable, a cassette deck, and an eight-track player. At this time, I had had Charlie buy a few eight-tracks for me, and with Ray's help, I had recorded one of my own downstairs on Mom's stereo. Because Moshe had an abundance of Jewish music that he had received as Bar Mitzvah gifts, his many cassettes gave me a lot of listening choices.

Chapter 18

More Music

Grant School's music teacher, Mr. Neal, was very interested in exposing us students to a great variety of music. Our fourth-grade song book happened to contain the Israeli children's song "Zum Gali Gali."

(To hear it sung, Google it or go here: https://www.youtube.com/watch?v=xrCJs3Ci81A)

At the beginning of the year, Mr. Neal played a recorded version of the song which had come with the master song book. I was able to participate in class by using a Braille copy of the song book. I had discovered that "Zum Gali Gali" was on page 129 of the song book. I had an idea; I wanted to see what Mr. Neal would do if I asked him to have the class sing "Zum Gali Gali."

The opportunity came on a day not too long after my suspension from the lunch table. That day, Mr. Neal was leaving it up to us to decide which songs we wanted to sing. Raising my hand to get his attention, I asked him if we could sing "the song on page 129." Advancing to it, he discovered that it was "Zum Gali Gali." He nearly started laughing, stating that he had never played the song before, but if I wanted to have the class do it, we would. I laughed, stating to him that the song was second nature for me to sing. In past class periods, he had sometimes played "Sunrise, Sunset" for the class, stating that he was doing it for me.

He instructed the other boys and girls in the room to sing the chorus, "Zum Gali Gali," and I would do the verses. We began to sing the song, and it took only one or two times for everybody to catch on. Mr. Neal then decided that the school choir should do the song, and he would let me be the one to sing solo verses, displaying the fact that I was Jewish. He told me after class that he wanted to see if there was another New Hebrew (modern Hebrew) song that I could sing.

A few days later, Mr. Neal approached me while I was eating in the lunchroom. Asking me if I knew the national anthem for the State of Israel, he was excited to hear me say, "Sure!" He explained that there was a song in the sixth–grade song book that was the English version of it. Immediately, he began rehearsing "Zum Gali Gali" and "Hatikva" with the choir, calling "Hatikva" the "National Anthem for the State of Israel." He then gave me a copy of the song book; I brought it home for Mom, so she could play the accompaniment with me as I practiced. Taking a look at the song, Ray discovered that the words were not a precise English translation of "Hatikva," but I decided not to say anything on the matter to Mr. Neal.

In the days that followed the choir's first rehearsal of "Zum Gali Gali," I would be sitting in the lunchroom eating when I would hear a bunch of black students suddenly begin singing, "Zum Gali Gali Gali, Zum Gali Gali." They began to get rowdy doing this and had to be quieted down by the on–duty staff. They also began doing this out on the playground. I was totally elated at having introduced this Hebrew song to a bunch of Gentiles.

Our school's spring concert, featuring presentations by our choir and band, took place on May 28th. The choir had also been rehearsing the songs "God Bless America" and "They Call It America." Mr. Neal decided that we would open the concert with "Zum Gali Gali." We would then sing "The National Anthem for the State of Israel," "God Bless America" (with audience participation), and "They Call It America." This concert was the last all–out concert of the year, and it was my first time performing with the advanced band.

Chapter 19

More Negative Life Lessons

The concert was a success. I was glowing about having sung my Hebrew solos—that is, until something happened toward the end of the school day that made me begin to question my personal identity. As I was walking upstairs with the class, a student who had gotten to know me was trying to introduce me to a friend of his. He told the person that I was Jewish, and the other student responded that he hated Jews. Unbelieving, I asked the other student, "Really?" The other student responded, "Yeah." I was shaken for a second and asked, "Why?" The student said, "I don't know," then moved away from me.

Remembering the morning's experience, I could not understand this. The matter left me feeling quite disturbed, to the point that I contracted a one-day bout of flu and missed school the next day. Although people had shouted insults to us from their windows as we walked the streets on Shabbos, I just did not understand how anybody in Dayton, Ohio could hate Jews that much. I knew that we as a nation had had many enemies throughout history, but I had always figured that not that many people hated us. If they did, there must be some basic reason why we were hated, possibly having to do with Jesus. After about a week, I figured that what this guy had said was no big deal, and that as long as the majority of Gentiles in Dayton did not hate us, then all was well.

***

That school year, I took swimming lessons after school in the nearby Princeton Recreational Center, which had been built the previous year. I got along great with all the instructors. It was other kids my age who stopped me from going there to swim on my own. After swimming, they would sneak up behind me in the locker room and hit me with wet towels. Whenever they spoke to me, I noticed strong, black dialect in their speech. I never thought that their being black had anything to do with their behavior to me in the Recreational Center's locker room; however, I knew I did not want to be bothered. Mom and Dad went back to taking me to Belmont Pool, located near Grant School, to swim during leisure time.

***

Once we moved into our own house, our family life changed in some ways. One aspect of this was that whenever Mom felt tired in the evening and didn't want to prepare supper, she and Dad would take us out to eat. With no kosher restaurants in Dayton, we resorted to eating fish sandwiches, French fries, pizza with no meat toppings, and vegetarian Chinese, Italian, Mexican, and Indian food in non-kosher restaurants and pizza parlors. At the time of our move, we did this nearly every other night for about two weeks. Then, as my fourth grade year took hold, we started doing this once a week or so.

The phrase that was always in circulation in our house about this matter was, "Don't tell." As we would step out of the car and walk up to the door of a restaurant, we would all figuratively hold our breath, hoping that nobody from Shomrei Emuna or any other synagogue would see us. The same also applied when we exited the restaurant. Sometimes, as I was eating a salad in a restaurant, I thought I heard the voices of various people in the Shul murmuring that they were watching us as we ate non-kosher food. Mom told me that we were safe and not to worry. At first, I thought this was fun. Here we were as a family, with Mom and Dad leading us in breaking the law in secrecy.

***

Up until this point in my life, I had always looked at the fun, positive side of things. I had always suspected that there could not possibly be a problem as severe as people made it out to be. I had assumed that somebody "on drugs" was on medication. Although Dad had been working part time in a drug center for several years, he rarely spoke about his work around the family. If he did speak about the damage that narcotics do to the body and brain, I was too young to understand what he was trying to explain. Mom had taken a job that school year working with young adults who had been on drugs. She described how their minds did not work right, and I took it to mean that the medication they were on was causing this problem.

One Friday toward the end of that school year, Dad had to stop at Project Cure, the drug center, to pick up his paycheck. He invited me to come into the building with him in order to introduce me to some of his coworkers and clients. Being somewhat curious about what went on in this "drug center," I gladly left the car and took his arm. He led me through the door into a small building. The building seemed to have small hallways and somehow felt disheveled. I was expecting the atmosphere in the building to be like that of a drugstore, with bottles and packets of various types of medication to be found on numerous shelves. Instead, Dad led me through a hallway to a room where people were sitting inside, seemingly waiting for something.

Dad knocked on the door of a room, and I assume it was a staff member who answered. We entered the room, and Dad immediately introduced me as his son. Just then, a black woman walked into the room; Dad said she was a client of his, and he introduced me to her. At this point, I understood that his clients were the people he worked with, trying to get them off drugs. The woman client began to make small talk with me, asking me friendly questions.

As Dad was being handed his paycheck, she decided to get my opinion of the building. "How do you like the building?" she asked.

My response was, "It's not what I had expected it would be in here."

"What did you think was here?"

I responded, "I thought I would find bottles of your medications laying around."

Everybody in the office began to laugh very loudly, as though I had told the funniest joke any of them had heard in years.

The woman client said, "Well, if it was a few years ago, you *would* have found bottles of my medication laying around. That's all over, babe."

It was then, at 11 years of age, that I realized that the drugs that people were "on" were not necessarily medication. There was another awakening for me, too, in that I began to realize that serious world problems also existed in the city I lived in. However, for the time being, I chose to walk out of Project Cure with Dad and not think about this. I had Shabbos to look forward to that night.

Chapter 20

Camp Stone's Lessons
and Lingering Effects

I had never spent a long time away from home before. However, I was very excited about going to Camp Stone during the upcoming summer. Camp Stone is an Israeli-oriented, religious Jewish camp in northern Pennsylvania, about two and a half hours east of Cleveland. I'll describe it in more detail later in my story.

Moshe was also going that summer, so I would not be going away from home all by myself. No doubt he would be in a cabin or whatever with older guys, but I was sure we would still see each other during various camp activities.

Moshe and I rode into Cleveland with the Blubaums, a fellow Shomrei Emuna family whose children had been attending this camp for a number of years. Dov, the father, took us out to lunch at Kinneret Kosher Restaurant in Cleveland before dropping us off with our luggage at the

Young Israel Synagogue and helping us get settled on the bus to Camp Stone.

It was during this session of camp that I finally began to understand about Jewish suffering. I had heard about the Holocaust in Sunday school and at other Jewish gatherings. I had heard that six million Jews had been killed by Hitler and the Nazis, but until this point, I did not understand the significance of that number or how the killings took place. I thought that the murders were only committed in Germany, and that the Nazis were only a small band of men who killed people much the same way muggers did on the streets. At times, I thought the number six million could have been some mistake, and that this was just some big deal Jews were making of the matter. Likewise, I had to learn the sad truth about the life of Jews in what was then the Soviet Union.

When I was a few years younger, I had heard Jews and people on the radio and TV talk about "Jews in the Soviet Union" so much that I thought Jews had it good there, and that Jews from all over the world were wishing they could be there, too. With all the big words that people used when talking about this subject, I had no way of understanding what they were talking about. As it was, I liked the sound of the two words, "Soviet Union," together. I would walk around the house saying the words repeatedly for no reason, until Moshe or Ray (usually Ray) stopped me out of annoyance. I could not understand what could be so wrong with those two words. Once, Moshe tried to explain to me that they treated Jews badly there. I was not convinced of this, as the subject kept coming up again and again in

Jewish settings and on the news. However, it was at this point that I was to be educated out of my mistaken thinking.

Moshe and I arrived at Camp Stone and were separated, going to our respective cabins. I was in the youngest boys' cabin and Moshe was in the oldest boys' cabin. It took less than an hour for me to become very close to my counselor, Nathan Bigman. I made up my mind that I would do every single thing he told me to do in order to have a good month with him and the rest of the camp attendees.

When the Fourth of July came around, I asked if there would be fireworks. Our family had always gone to see fireworks displays and be part of the crowd on the Fourth of July. With the little vision I had, I enjoyed the sight of what looked to me like falling lights. When I inquired of a woman staff member there, she responded, "The Fourth of July is a goyishe holiday, and there will be no fireworks in camp." I was a little upset by this, but chose not to let my feelings be known.

I had turned down the idea of bringing tzitzis (also spelled tzitzit) to camp, even though Mom said it was required. I had given up wearing them five years back, in preschool, when they had begun to interfere with my using the bathroom. One day after swimming, Nathan discovered that I was not wearing them, and he immediately provided me with a pair. I put on the pair he gave me and wore them every day following, for the rest of the session and beyond. As I began to wear the tzitzis, I began to think wholeheartedly about everything I did back in Dayton that might not have been allowed according to Jewish law. Consequently, I began to feel uncomfortable with the idea of eating pizza and other food out with the family again in Dayton.

On Tisha B'Av, we were all mandated to watch a movie that was based on a true account of a Norwegian family who had survived the Holocaust. This movie contained dialog which spoke of every aspect of the Holocaust: the Germans conducting house searches, rounding Jews up, concentration camps, gas chambers, and crematoriums. This was the first that I had heard of the last three. It was also the first that I had heard of Germans having been in other countries during the war on their rampage to kill the Jews.

There was no discussion following this movie. I felt as if I needed to speak to somebody about the facts that I had just learned. I let it go, though, thinking that I would find out more about the Holocaust as time went on. However, I still had to learn about the current and most prevalent instance of Jewish suffering at this time: the fate of our brethren living in the Soviet Union.

There were six Russian campers at Camp Stone that month. Two of them were in my cabin. I noticed early in the session that all six of the Russian campers knew next to nothing about Judaism. I also noticed that one of the Russian boys seemed to be in rather bad health. On the next–to–last night of the session, one of the Americans in my cabin asked one of the Russians a question about life in Russia. Both boys told sad stories of their family life in Russia and about how hard it was there for Jews. It took me quite a long time to fall asleep after that. I left Camp Stone in a rather bewildered state. From then on, I knew that when people spoke of Russia or the Soviet Union, they were usually referring to the same place.

By the end of the session, I had had a good month of swimming, horseback riding, sliding down the land and water omegas of the camp, and much more worthwhile recreation and games. However, I felt uncomfortable leaving the camp, sure that there was more about the Holocaust and Soviet Jewry that I should know about. I was to turn 12 at the end of October—which meant that my Bar Mitzvah was roughly one year away.

I realized that it was time for me to learn more about my people as a nation as they exist today. However, I felt strange asking people to whom I was not as close as family about these matters. I felt that I could talk to Mom about these matters, at least up to a point. However, I still chose not to talk to her too much about them, as I felt that I should not have been as bothered by them as I was. I felt that Dad was almost never in a state of mind in which he could fully listen to me.

At Camp Stone, I had become accustomed to attending prayer services three times a day. Several times before I went to Camp Stone, I had forgotten to pray Shacharis in my rush to get out of the house and to school. At the tail end of the session, I vowed to make an extra effort to daven (to pray) at the proper time, no matter what the cost.

When the session at Camp Stone concluded, Moshe and I rode the bus with the other campers from Cleveland

and other cities at points west back to the Young Israel Synagogue in Cleveland, where our parents were waiting eagerly to pick us up. I apprehensively walked off the bus and stood dumbfounded for a second. Then Mom came over and threw her arms around me. Feeling sorry that I had to admit to her that I had taken a more religious direction, I thought I should warn her. My first words to her were, "I've got bad news, Mom. I've become frum." I thereupon explained what had happened with Nathan and the tzitzis. This would not have been bad news if I could have been a little more independent from the family. I was still at a young enough age that I could very easily be drawn into whatever the rest of the family did.

I tried to go about my life in this new manner of thinking, but I found it hard. Although Mom and Dad chose to eat out less than before, they still did it on some nights when even I did not feel like eating what was in the house. I kept vowing that I would not go out with them to eat, but at the last minute, I would decide to. In tears, I would go into my bedroom and remove my tzitzis. After joining the family, I would say a silent prayer that God might understand that I had not chosen this.

My learning with David Tishbaum was still going on at this time. As I neared my twelfth birthday, he began to talk to me about the significance of being a Bar Mitzvah. He now began to tell me that once I was a Bar Mitzvah, any single action, good or bad, would make a tremendous difference with what happened to the entire Jewish people. A few times, he touched on the subject of the Holocaust. He told me that as long as every Jew who knows how to keep the Torah does so, it will never happen again, but it can and will happen again if people do things they are not supposed to. This made me feel even more guilty each time I ate out with the rest of the family. As far as what would happen in future years is concerned, I feel it is best to say that compromises have to be made by everybody at some point in their lives, and that things work out in the end.

I joined the Boy Scouts the week after my return from Camp Stone. In truth, I did that mainly on Dad's suggestion. However, I think it is fair to say that I did gain a certain exposure to the unknown that I would not have otherwise had.

Chapter 21

Shoshanna

One Friday in August, as I was wheeling my bicycle down the driveway to have a ride on the sidewalk, I heard something whimpering to me, asking for my attention. I figured that it was a puppy or small dog. I was not sure if I should reach down and touch it, for fear that it might bite. I stood at the bottom of the driveway, not knowing what to do. Then this puppy, or whatever it was, seemed to be able to sense my blindness, and it came over to me and began to nuzzle my shoes. I had the feeling that I was safe and reached down and began to pet it. It was a puppy!

I had the feeling that Mom did not wish to adopt another stray dog after our experience with Tippy. However, I could sense that this puppy needed food and thought I could give it some food and send it away. I turned and advanced my bicycle up the driveway, and the puppy followed me. I walked into the house and got Mom's attention.

Mom immediately took note of the puppy, which was lovingly following me around. She put food and water down for it and let it eat. Then we took the puppy into the other room to investigate. Looking at the underside, Mom determined it was a female. Moshe and I then walked up the street, asking neighbors who were standing out if this puppy was theirs. Nobody claimed ownership, so we decided to adopt her. Because of her loving quality, which I considered to be as sweet as the scent of a flower, we named her Shoshanna, which is Hebrew for rose. A few weeks later, Mom took Shoshanna to the vet. The vet determined that she was part Siberian Husky and part German Shepherd. She had to be given shots for worms.

Shoshanna was loving to just about everybody during the year and a half that followed, even though there were a few people in the neighborhood who were frightened of her. Sometimes if the telephone company people were in the neighborhood, they would stop off at our house just to pet Shoshanna. In my opinion, she was an extremely smart dog. Without any training, she instinctively knew to stop when Moshe or I came to a street corner during walks. If I was about to lose my balance or she felt I was coming too close to the street, she would brace her body in an effort to keep me safe. When I would come in from the cold, she would jump on me and hug me until she was sure I was warm once again. She instinctively knew how cold a person's hands got during the winter. As she hugged, she would rub herself against the hands, trying to warm them up. There is much else that I could say in her praise, but we must now return to the background of the story ahead.

A little over a week after Shoshanna's arrival, the cornea of my right eye began to scar down. Mom found a local pediatric ophthalmologist who was eager to help us in any way he could. After doing some research, he gave a tentative diagnosis of Moshe's and my hereditary condition: Leber's Congenital Amarosis. For confirmation of this, tests were run on every member of the immediate family and Uncle Bobby the following December on the Ohio State University campus in Columbus. Although a few doctors got a lot of good research in, I lost some usable vision at this point. I could no longer use the closed circuit TV, and it was determined that I would need to learn cane travel that upcoming school year. Our diagnosis of Leber's Congenital Amarosis was disproved by a local neurologist nearly 26 years later.

Chapter 22

Fifth-Grade Woes

In some ways, my fifth-grade year was worse than my third-grade year. I would venture to say that it was almost a waste. Like my third-grade class, my fifth-grade class had an overabundance of unruly students in it. Some of them had been in my third-grade class; I recognized their names from roll call. Fortunately, Teresa Hargess was in this class and remembered me.

I still had no understanding of child abuse and unhappy families. I had no way of understanding why I could be attacked for no reason by people younger than me. Just as in third grade, I would sometimes return home from school crying from the negative emotional impact of the other students, which was far from anything I knew at home.

There were several days when I did next to nothing in the classroom. Having just joined the Boy Scouts, I took the opportunity of reading the Boy Scout Manual during the day when the teacher, Mrs. Foreman, could not control the class. Eventually, as long as I was reading, she said that I was doing schoolwork. Even if I was reading a Braille book with leisure content, she counted it as classwork.

Mrs. Foreman was black, with a strong dialect which differed from those of Mrs. Baker or Mrs. Wilkinson. Considering the fact that she was a teacher, she seemed to have rather limited education. However, her loving disposition made up for that. There were aspects of her personality which puzzled me. Sometimes she would refer to herself in the third person, telling everybody in the classroom that "Mrs. Foreman doesn't feel good." Usually, when she did this, she would take out some sort of candy and begin eating it in front of the class. I remember privately and silently questioning her abilities as a teacher, but liking and respecting her all the same.

With the arrival of winter, the students in the classroom became more and more rambunctious. Sometimes when I was in the middle of writing one of our very few assignments, a student would walk up to me and pinch me, then run away. Becoming sick and tired of this routine, I decided to fight back. A few times when I was pinched or tagged, I reached out my hand to strike. Usually I would fall on the floor next to the desk and feel like a fool. Two times when I was pinched, I reached out my left hand and grabbed the clothing of the guilty person. He ran across the room, dragging me like a sack of booty—as the entire class, with the exception of Teresa and a few other students, roared with laughter. Mrs. Foreman tried to stop the students and discipline them, but it was to no avail. Eventually, the taunters took to throwing spitballs around the classroom nonstop. Fortunately, they did not do this to me too often, but chose to antagonize me in other ways. They began to sneak up on me and pull on my clothing, exposing my tzitzis and undershirt.

That year, Ms. Hild taught the blind class in the resource room of the school. In addition, the Braille Library Service installed a specialized recorded version of the *World Book Encyclopedia*. Ms. Hild took great delight in showing me how to do research using the special cassettes and player. She told me I was welcome to come in and use the encyclopedia during any spare time when nothing important was going on in Mrs. Foreman's room. Eventually, when I had had enough of the other students' disorderly conduct and bullying, I would ask Mrs. Foreman if I could go to "the other room." She always said yes. I think she realized that I was trying to escape her class, but she knew that it was for my benefit to do so.

Finally, in early March, action had to be taken when a few students began to shove me in my private area. After Dad and Mom came in and bargained with Mr. Nilson, I was switched to the resource room and had special subjects such as art, gym, and music with the sixth grade. I was shown a different restroom downstairs to use instead of the one near Ms. Hild's room. She had taken note of the reason for my being moved and feared that I could still be harassed by former classmates who might spot me in the restroom. I realized after the fact that this was the same restroom we had used in preschool.

My start in the resource room occurred just after spring vacation. In my last conversation with Mrs. Foreman, she made me promise her that if Mr. Nilson asked me anything about the class, I would not blame anything on her. I promised. Mr. Nilson never questioned me, but I found out years later that Mrs. Foreman was fired from teaching at the end of that school year.

Once in the resource room, Ms. Hild allowed me to work through my textbooks at my own pace, doing assignments that I thought looked challenging enough. I felt privileged to be working at my own real level, but somehow felt as though I was cheating—or that I was being cheated by the educational system.

It was in this latter part of the school year that Mr. Alan taught me cane travel. From the first time Dad and Mom saw me using a cane on the streets, they insisted that I use it whenever I left the house. Mom would even get upset at times when I attempted to leave the house without it.

That school year, I played trumpet in advanced band during the entire school year. The teacher was Mr. Molon. For the first time, I went to concertize in other schools. This gave me a feeling of importance, but I felt as though I needed more direction in how to perfect my skill at playing. This became more pronounced when Mr. Molon gave me a solo to practice and perform. I kept messing up in performance out of nervousness. Private lessons were soon to follow.

Very often that school year and beyond, my mind was continuously focusing on the situation of Jews in the Soviet

Union—or Russia, as I thought of it. I wondered if there was anything I could do about their situation. Once, somebody gave me the idea of writing letters to these Jews. Although I happened to enjoy writing letters more than most boys my age, I felt so sorry for the people that I didn't know what to say to them. As it was, something about my life seemed to resemble theirs. I felt as though I could somehow identify with these people. In my mind, letters were not enough. I felt that something more should be done toward the salvation of these Jews. This matter would sometimes keep me up very late at night. I had many nights when sleep was nearly impossible, as I could not stop thinking about how Jews were being tortured in a far off place, and I could do nothing about it.

When I would get up out of bed in the small hours of the morning, I would inadvertently wake up Dad. He would come out of his room and begin yelling at me, insisting that I was only asking for attention by being up. I had been planning to sit down with Dad one day and talk about this, but always felt him to be unapproachable. It began to seem to me that at times, in his own way, he acted like one of those Soviet Union leaders. I could not understand why it was so hard for him to listen to me when I tried to tell him that I honestly could not sleep.

Nevertheless, despite these occurrences, I felt that Dad was on my side in more than one way. As my twelfth year on earth progressed, I began to think that somehow, some way, I would be able to gain Dad's favor after my Bar Mitzvah and he would gladly listen to what I wished to talk with him about.

***

My fifth–grade school year ended on a somewhat depressing note. Matt Chaney had a brain tumor, and he was becoming more mentally deficient with each passing week. From the time we had been in Mrs. Wilkinson's class together, I had known that he had seizures. When he had one, he would fall on the floor and go into a deep slumber that nobody could get him out of. Either his mother or a paramedic would have to come and carry him out of the building. Now it was obvious to me that he was wasting away. After going through a period in the classroom when he would say nonsensical things to himself, all he could do was make noises that made him sound like a zoo animal. We students and staff members who knew Matt from before were greatly saddened by this.

For the last few months of that school year, Ms. Hild had to spend a lot of extra time preparing lessons for the other students. Sometimes she would ask me to hold off on handing in assignments for her to grade. She would often let me spend entire mornings or afternoons doing research with the recorded *World Book*, or she would allow me to put on headphones and do recreational listening to children's and young adult library records. Going to school had become fun and boring at the same time. Finally the school year came to an end, and that finished my time at Grant School.

Chapter 23

A New School and New Challenges

That summer was somewhat restful, with the exception of my first major asthma attack. It happened one July evening during the three weeks when all doctors' offices were closed. Terror-stricken, I lay on a bed unable to breathe, sure that I had pneumonia. Mom called our doctor's office, but Dr. Collins, our family doctor (an internist), could not be reached. Mom then tried to call another doctor who was unwilling to come to his office for any reason. He attempted to prescribe medication over the phone. Mom was unwilling to take any chances, given that this doctor refused to get a diagnosis first. She stayed by my bedside in the living room that long night while I barely slept. Early next morning, we called and made an appointment with Dr. Collins. He diagnosed my condition as asthma and prescribed appropriate medication after giving me a shot.

Up to this point, you may be thinking that I am Job the Second. Don't worry; I'm not. Despite the hard times at school, many nice things also happened during those years. In addition to those two family trips to Florida and other trips to Milwaukee as I grew older, there were many happy holiday gatherings to be remembered for years to come. There were also two trips to the Ohio State Fair, as well as many outings in the woods. For Moshe and me, spending time with the Goldmans in Milwaukee was for the most part boring. However, some of the car trips to and from were full of adventure. All of us loved eating kosher meals at the Falafel King in Skokie.

I knew that upon entering Hillel Academy, I could expect more homework and higher demands from teachers. I had visited Hillel Academy a few times during the previous school year. Although my classmates to be seemed very welcoming to me, I was under the impression that they could easily turn on me for one reason or another once I was enrolled as a student there—which, as you will see, turned out to be true. However, prior to entering Hillel Academy, I was not going to let this bother me. After all, I had waited a long time to be in a Jewish school, and I wanted to make the best of it. What I was unaware of was that many of these students were only attending Hillel Academy in order to be Bar and Bat Mitzvahed in their synagogue, or their parents did not want them attending Dayton public schools. All I cared about at the time was that I could supposedly finally obtain a religious education. Unfortunately, the odds were not in my favor on this matter.

Sixth grade began, and I found myself struggling with expectations I had never imagined. Hillel Academy had a double program of Hebrew and English subjects. The English subjects were taught at an entire grade level above that in the public schools. Coming from a scholastic situation the previous year in which I had barely been learning anything, I had to get myself re-accustomed to a traditional classroom setup, and there were the higher expectations on top of that. My English-language subjects that year included English grammar, literature, social studies, science, and math. Our gym teacher came into our classroom and taught health twice a week.

Mrs. Portworth taught three of my six English-language subjects: literature, English grammar, and social studies. I found many of the stories in our literature textbook to be far above any story that I had read back at Grant School. Many nights in a row, Mrs. Portworth would assign four very intensive grammar exercises and one of these stories as homework. Mrs. Norris, who taught math and science, also did her fair share of assigning homework. However, she was seemingly more merciful than Mrs. Portworth. It was normal for a student to feel pressured by Mrs. Portworth. Back at home, Dad explained to me several times that the teachers were trying to prepare these other students to get into good colleges. However, both he and Mom were very upset that I had to stay up as late as midnight to finish the majority of my homework. Even so, it was not uncommon for me to go to bed without finishing some important assignments.

That year, my Judaic subjects consisted of Hebrew

grammar, Chumash, Mishna, and Prophets. Our Hebrew grammar teacher was a non–observant American Jewish woman who had spent a lot of time living in Israel. Her marriage in the middle of the year meant that the class had to go from calling her Ms. Sarlson to calling her Mrs. Fadlawn. As the year progressed, she became more and more impatient with us students. However, I was able to slightly improve my spoken Hebrew with her help.

Our Bible and Mishna teacher was Rabbi Pelberg. He had just moved from New York in hopes of making a living and raising a family in Dayton. He had been hired to teach at Hillel Academy, but in reality, from the start, his main intention had been to make his livelihood from working with computers. Very often, it was his Mishna and Samuel worksheets that were neglected from my homework until the fourth quarter. I was just shy of failing his subjects until he discovered that I was really trying my best for him.

Among various other subjects that Rabbi Pelberg taught and spoke about was the Holocaust. He used a special textbook which we were able to order from the Jewish Braille Institute Braille Library. He also brought in testimonial films. My hair would stand on end when he taught and discussed this subject.

Art and music classes were held in the same classroom by two different teachers on different days of the week. Our art teacher was an everyday woman who did not feel that she needed to push us particularly hard. Our music teacher was a recent Jewish immigrant from the Soviet Union who unfortunately was not respected by most students in my class.

That year, Cantor Kopmar put me in Chamber Choir. I was somewhat arrogant about being in Chamber Choir until one of my classmates set me straight.

Cantor Kopmar still did not accept me into Tour Choir that year. He told me that he had almost accepted me, but he thought I should mature a bit more first. He promised me that should there be a tour the following year, he would not hesitate to let me go on it. He did allow me to go on a mini-tour to Detroit with the choir over Presidents' Day Weekend, which was a lot of fun.

My Bar Mitzvah occurred during this school year. It took place at Shomrei Emuna on November 7, 1981. For two weeks prior to the Bar Mitzvah, Mom and other women of the Shul worked like mad to organize and then put together a delicious Shabbos lunch to be served after services that morning. Rabbi Katz, our rabbi at the time, was having his second year as rabbi of Congregation Shomrei Emuna. I was his first Bar Mitzvah. He and Dad helped me prepare a meaningful speech to give to the congregation and guests that morning.

I turned 13 on the Hebrew calendar at nightfall of the Wednesday preceding the Bar Mitzvah. I could not sit still as Rabbi Katz spoke between Minchah and Maariv. I kept walking into the kitchen to telephone Time and Temperature in order to find out whether or not I was a man by Jewish law. Finally, Dad sat me down and calmly told me to relax. He assured me that Rabbi Katz would let us know. Sure enough, Dad was right. At the conclusion of his speaking, Rabbi Katz wasted no time. "Now, we will daven, and the person who was not a Bar Mitzvah when he came in here this evening is now." He then commanded me to walk up to the Bimah and begin to lead the congregation in Maariv.

I led the davenning for Maariv that night with a special zeal. Upon my successfully completing the service, everybody crowded around me to shake my hand and wish me mazol tov. The entire congregation began to sing and dance. David Tishbaum lifted me on his shoulders as he sang and danced with great fervor.

Next day, I found school to be quite overwhelming. That evening, Dad said I would not be going to school the next day, because that would be the day before my Bar Mitzvah. He assured me that many Jewish boys skip school the day before the Bar Mitzvah.

That evening, Ray, who had enrolled himself at the New School for Social Research in New York City, flew back to Columbus on the People's Express. Dad drove in to get him. While he was gone, Naomi Ranan arrived by cab from the airport. She had my tefillin with her. They had been made especially for me by a relative of a Dayton family whom I knew vaguely at the time.

The following morning, Sue Goldman flew in from Milwaukee. Charlie, who worked weekends at the time and attended Ohio State University, or OSU, came in sometime during Friday afternoon. Moshe skipped school that day. I could not understand his doing this, as he did not skip school the day before his own Bar Mitzvah. By Shabbos, the entire family, including Uncle Bobby, was at the house.

That Friday evening, for the first time ever, I led Kabalas Shabbos and Maariv, which followed. I was greatly complimented by several people in the Shul thereafter. Many people asked me if I was nervous. In truth, I was only slightly nervous, because I realized I had the potential to do a good job. I told everybody who asked that I was not nervous.

That night at dinner, there were more people seated around our dining room table than I could remember ever having been there before. In fact, I believe that Mom and Dad had to set up an extra table and chairs in the living room. Some families who did not keep Shabbos were staying in the area nearby in order to attend my Bar Mitzvah next day. Again, people asked me if I was nervous, and I gave them the same response. When they asked me how I was feeling in general, I told them I was feeling fine, if not better than ever before.

For my Bar Mitzvah next morning, I led Shacharis and Musaf and chanted the week's Haftara after getting an Aliyah. Mr. Lischt, the Shul treasurer and candy man, had taken great delight in training me and was thrilled with my performance.

All the girls from my class at Hillel Academy had come to the Bar Mitzvah. A few of the boys came as well. Ms. Hild and a few other Gentiles who were good friends of the family came to Shomrei Emuna for the occasion. After the service, we all crowded into the small Shul kitchen for Kiddush, which was to be followed by lunch.

With so many people there, we could not all eat in one part of the Shul. I sat in the back of the basement with Rabbi Katz on my left and Mr. Lischt on my right. I felt greatly honored to be sitting in between these two people.

I had requested that Mrs. Lischt make cholent (a type of stew) for this occasion. Everybody loved her cholent. We also had cold cuts that had been brought in from Cincinnati. The entire affair was a success. To this day, that was the time when I felt the proudest of myself.

Around Channukkah, Ray came home on vacation and gave me a Bar Mitzvah present. I had expressed to him an interest in seeing a synthesizer and possibly even owning one someday. He went to an antique shop and bought me a $60 Casio keyboard. It was a little over a foot long and had a pouch and very tiny keys. It had a piano sound, a guitar sound, an electrical sound, an organ sound, a violin sound, and an option to create your own instrument. The keyboard also had a calculator feature, which was unusable to me. What was the most exciting was that you could record your own melody into the keyboard. There were also various beats to choose from. I had the feeling that someday I would own something bigger and better than this, but I cherished this keyboard. I was very grateful to Ray for a long time for having bought me my first synthesizer–like toy keyboard.

Chapter 24

Losing Shoshanna

The first weekend of the following January, we lost Shoshanna. This is how it happened.

The Baschs were spending Shabbos in the area; they were eating at our house and sleeping at Shomrei Emuna. That weekend, both Charlie and Ray were home. After supper on Friday night, Mom and Dad asked Charlie and Ray to walk the Baschs back to Shomrei Emuna. As they left the house, Dad climbed the stairs to bed. Moments later, Mom got an idea. She decided to let Shoshanna out of the house, loose. She would track down Charlie and Ray and walk with them. She was totally trustworthy without a leash by this point. Charlie and Ray had both requested that Mom not send her along. Mom thought that neither of them would actually mind, so she went ahead and sent Shoshanna out without a leash.

About 45 minutes later, Mom was reading a story to Moshe and me in the living room when Charlie walked into the house with blood on his hands. Painfully, he relayed the sad tale of what had just happened. Shoshanna had found them and the Baschs, and they had gotten as far as Shomrei Emuna. Once they were inside, Charlie and Ray decided to do some extra walking in the area. As they headed up Salem Avenue, one of Dayton's most dangerous streets, Shoshanna decided to play a game with them. She kept running across the street when there were no cars coming, then waiting until the next free moment to come running back to Charlie and Ray. One of those times when she was running back, a van hit her but did not knock her out. However, it slowed her movement and reaction time. Next, two or three other cars hit her and sent her body moving toward Charlie and Ray.

Charlie said he pulled her out of the street by her tail. A kind person gave Charlie and Ray a ride back home and they set Shoshanna, nearly dead, to rest in peace by a favorite tree of hers in our wooded lot next to our house. I had a lot of trouble sleeping that night and went into Dad and Mom's bedroom at around 4:00 in the morning to talk. When Dad heard the news of what had happened, he began to yell at Mom for not putting a leash on Shoshanna. He went downstairs and outside to investigate the situation, and that only made his anger worse. If I recall correctly, he did not sleep for the rest of that night.

All through the rest of Shabbos, we mourned Shoshanna. What did not help was the temperature going down as far as 20 degrees below zero. Even now, Shoshanna lives in our hearts and minds as a loving legend of a dog. No dog I have ever known will ever compare to her.

Chapter 25

Regrets and Mistreatment

By midyear at Hillel Academy, I had begun to regret that I had enrolled there. With the amount of homework issued by the teachers, I found that I barely had any time for myself. As far as religious learning was concerned, I was not learning as much as I had hoped for. Rabbi Pelberg seemed to be too preoccupied to give me necessary personal attention.

My classmates could not stand my wearing my yarmulke, or kipa, as they called it, when we went on field trips. I was shocked by this, given that I had never had any problem wearing it when I went on field trips with Gentiles. As my classmates pleaded with me to remove it, I stood my ground and refused. When they insisted that people were spitting on them, I responded that if people were going to spit on them, they would have to spit on me, too, because I was the one wearing the kipa. And as long as

I was not being spat on, I would not take it off. Eventually, I grew to dread going outside of the school with my class. Fortunately, there were not many field trips during my time at Hillel Academy.

To make matters worse, I began to be physically intimidated by a few of my classmates. It was not as bad as what I had suffered the year before at Grant School, but it was enough to make me dread any minute of free time with the class. Two students in particular seemed to have a need to sneak up from behind and kick me in the shins or hit me on the back. A few times, I fought back. However, as this persisted, the emotional impact of what was happening to me in school began to change my overall mood and perception of the world around me.

During this one and only complete school year at Hillel Academy, there was a new disciplinary system they were trying out in the local school systems. If a student was inattentive or disorderly in any way, their name would be written by the current teacher on the chalkboard. If they continued to misbehave, they were given a check mark. A student would receive this same punishment if he or she forgot a textbook or did not do his or her homework. Once, I was out sick on a Friday and did not learn that an assignment was due on Monday. I received a check mark and had to eat lunch outside the cafeteria. But believe it or not, that was fun. I was forced to buy my lunch from the cafeteria and then take it to the art room, to eat with other students who were getting the same punishment.

Ed, the janitor, was the most easygoing person in the school at that time. He was set over us to watch us. He kept cracking jokes about our behavior, which only proved that none of us were that bad.

The reward a person could work up to was eating lunch with Dr. Kleiner, the current principal of the school. I always saw Dr. Kleiner (may he rest in peace) as a very boring and somber man. As a matter of fact, I had a hard time paying attention to him when he addressed the school. Thus I was never sad that I could not work up to this "reward."

Chapter 26

A New Fascination with Faraway Places

That school year, I developed a strange, sudden curiosity about New York City. Actually, I had been wondering about life there for a few years already. Mom had told me about memories of her childhood in Brooklyn, but I assumed that things there had probably changed a lot since then. In the midst of the turmoil brought on by my experiences at Hillel Academy, I was thinking about other large U.S. cities quite a lot at that time. I had never been to most of these cities, but I had heard about them in the media and from other people who had been there. In light of my interest in and curiosity about New York City, Mom decided that she and I would make a special trip there sometime in the next few years.

I also thought a lot about certain foreign countries that I had either heard of or was learning about in social studies. In social studies, we were learning about the lives of people in European countries over the past few centuries. It was during that school year, while attempting to do some homework, that I finally figured out how to read our Braille atlas, which was originally purchased for Moshe. I began to be fascinated by several maps, particularly those of the British Isles, Germany, and the Soviet Union, as well as various maps of the Middle East, including Israel. I thought that Poland was a neat shape in a neat location—sandwiched between East Germany on its left and the Soviet Union on its right.

I also enjoyed our maps of the U.S. I would feel my map of Manhattan time and time again, imagining that I was there. I memorized every river and every bridge associated with it. I purposely sought out which rivers led to which other boroughs of New York City. I also memorized my maps of New York State, thinking I should know everything I could about the state that New York City was a part of.

Naturally, I was a little envious of Moshe, who went on tour with the choir that year to Toronto (in Ontario, Canada) and to New York City. However, I had high hopes that I would be going on tour the following year.

My tension increased as spring approached. Around Pesach, I began to have dreams in the early mornings which seemed to be simulations of what I had been learning about the Holocaust. Not all these dreams were the same, but they had the same basic content. Sometimes I would be captured in our house, then taken and put on a bus with other Jews and taken away to an unknown location. Ironically, when I was placed on these buses and was forced to ride, it was in the same manner that I usually sat and rode a bus going to and from school. I would be seated in a seat all by myself—hearing other people around me but not feeling that I was a part of them or had anything whatsoever to do with them.

Other dreams would start in the other location. Usually, they would end in a shower room as a door closed. In the dreams, I knew what to expect: gas. There were only a few dreams in which I was able to escape. At the time, I had feelings of shame about this. To the best of my knowledge, no relatives of ours had been affected by the Holocaust. I continued having dreams of this type well into summer vacation. The only three people I felt I could tell about the dreams were Moshe, Mom, and Dad. Dad thought these dreams were related to my experiences at Hillel Academy. Fortunately, I had a month at Camp Stone to look forward to that summer.

Chapter 27

Camp Stone Again

Seventh Grade

Camp Stone that summer was somewhat different than two years earlier. I chose to go for the second session that summer, having heard that more kids would be going then and that the second session would probably be more exciting than the first one. Although I was 13, thus old enough to be placed in the oldest boys' cabin, they put me in the middle cabin because I was just out of sixth grade. I felt this to be unfair, but decided not to make an issue of it. After all, I got along great with most of my bunkmates from the moment I met them in Cleveland outside of the Young Israel Synagogue.

My counselor that summer was Shlomo Starchell. I could tell that he had come from an observant background, but he did not seem to be as strict about people keeping religious law as Nathan Bigman or Akiva Turk, who was the man running the camp that summer.

That summer, I was a big hit there with my trumpet. As soon as they discovered I could play, the heads of the camp worked my playing into various camp activities—especially playing along with the music teacher at supper. I helped her out in putting on the Zimria, or Song Festival, during the third week of camp. I came home in late August without even 24 hours to spare before the start of my seventh-grade year at Hillel Academy.

Although the classmates who had been attacking me physically and verbally had let up some toward the end of the previous year, it was obvious to me that they really and truly did not want me back. There were only two people who I was certain wanted me back in class with them. A number of those classmates of mine were Bar or Bat Mitzvahed during the early part of that school year. I attended a few of their parties at the Meadowbrook Country Club.

For the first half of that school year at Hillel Academy, my class went to a different classroom for each class instead of having the teacher come to us, the way it had been the year before. This was the first school year that I had to walk to each of my classes. In years past, the only classes I had had to walk to were gym, art, music, home economics, and the special skills training that I needed as a blind student. That half school year, English-language subjects included English, literature, Chinese history, Ohio history, math, science, and health. Subjects taught in Hebrew included Hebrew grammar (taught by a very nice

Israeli woman), Talmud (taught by Rabbi Pelberg), Jewish history, and Chumash. Jewish history was taught by Rabbi Rosenbaum. He was new in the community and could not maintain the slightest bit of control of any class. Chumash was taught by Rabbi Avraham Feld, Congregation Shomrei Emuna's newly inaugurated rabbi.

As usual, I had gym, art, and music this half school year. In gym, the teacher, Mr. Autin, did little more than give me a jump rope and have me jump the whole period, or have me try to see how many pushups I could do, while my classmates played ball.

Although Hillel Academy was in one of the smallest school buildings that I knew of in the city, it felt overwhelming to me. I began to get lost in the halls as I tried to make it from one class to the next. As the fall progressed, my absences due to sickness began to increase at a steady rate.

During the first half of the school year, Rabbi Pelberg attempted to teach our class a combination of Talmud and knowledge about computers on what was supposed to be an alternating basis. There was no way that I could work with computers at this point, as nobody involved knew anything about adaptive computer software and equipment for the blind. Originally, we were supposed to have designated days of the week to study Talmud, and the other days left over would be for computers. Teaching us about computers was somewhat more technical than Rabbi Pelberg had expected, and it became necessary to spend more time on the computers than on Talmud. I was elated, as this gave me extra time to do homework. On the other hand, I felt as though I was being cheated out of the religious education that I had waited all my life for. As it was, the Talmud was hardly even understandable to me.

With the number of times I missed school and came late to class, Mrs. Ross, the guidance councilor, decided to have some private conferences with me in her trailer office. She could not understand why going to school at Hillel Academy had been so hard for me and was not becoming any easier. She insisted that all my classmates were "normal young people around my age." She also stated, time and time again, that other students had come from Russia and Israel and had been able to adapt just fine—and if *they* could, there was no reason why *I* should not be able to.

As winter progressed, it became more and more obvious to Dad and Mom that I had to leave Hillel Academy. At that point, I was just beginning to think that I could call Hillel Academy my school, despite how I felt about attending there. I was not to know that Dad and Mom were talking about my leaving Hillel Academy until the point at which my main story begins, when an alternative arrangement had already been made.

At that time, my weekly allowance was $2.00. I had taken an old peanut butter jar from a kitchen cabinet and had set it aside for "New York savings." I began to put half of my allowance into this container every other week. As time went on, half of my allowance went in every week. When the jar was full of dollar bills, Mom took me to the bank and put the money in. Then I began the saving process over again. With Mom's help, I began to collect used aluminum foil, empty soda cans, and old newspapers for recycling in hopes of getting just a little extra money for our trip.

To be continued in Book Two.

Glossary of Jewish Terms and Concepts

Editor's Note:

The definitions of terms and the bracketed pronunciation guidelines were supplied by the author. The latter are not strictly phonetic.

Aba [ah-ba]

Hebrew, Father.

Adar [ah-dar]

The fifth month on the Hebrew calendar. Purim is the 14th day of this month.

Adon Olam [ah-doan o-lum]

A prayer often sung as a hymn at the end of synagogue services, which acknowledges God's sovereignty in the world and a Jew's trust in him.

Aliyah [ah-lee-ah]

1. A person's being called up to the front of the synagogue to stand next to the person reading the Torah for a specific section being read.

2. When a Jew makes his permanent home in Israel.

Amidah [a–mee–dah]

Prayer which takes the place of Shemoneh Esrei on Shabbos and holidays.

Aphikoman [ah–fee–ko–mun]

The larger half of the middle of three Matzahs at a Passover Seder. It is often hidden by children and eaten as the conclusion of the meal section of the Seder. It is a commemoration of the Passover sacrifice that was carried out in the Temple.

Aufrauf [uhf–ruhf]

A celebration held in a groom's synagogue the Shabbos preceding his wedding.

Baal Teshuvah [bahl teh–shoovah]

A person who was born into a non–observant background who comes to the faith and begins observing Orthodox Jewish law later in life.

Bachur [buh–kuhr]; plural, Bachurim [buh–kuhr–eem]

Yeshiva student.

Bar Mitzvah [bar mitzvuh]

1. The ceremony in which a Jewish boy who has just turned 13 years of age is called up to lead services and read from the Torah for the first time. This includes the celebration which follows.

2. The boy who is the celebrant of such an occasion.

3. Any Jewish male from his 13th Hebrew birthday and beyond.

Bat Mitzvah [baht mitzvuh]

1. Ceremony and party comparable to a Bar Mitzvah, only performed by a Jewish girl who has reached her 12th birthday. Twelve years of age is the point at which a Jewish girl reaches womanhood.

2. The girl who is the celebrant of such an occasion.

3. Any Jewish female from the time of her 12th Hebrew birthday and beyond.

Bedika [buh–dee–kuh]

Hebrew for *search*. Most often, the search of a home for leavened food, usually conducted the night before Passover.

Beit Keneset [bayt ke–nes–set]

Hebrew for *house of meeting*. Used to refer to a synagogue; place where people pray.

Bensch [bench]; Bensching

Grace after meals; recited if one has begun a meal by washing for bread. Also known as *Birkat HaMazon*.

Beracha [brah–khah]

A blessing. Also a girl's name.

Bimah [bee–muh]

The platform in a synagogue chapel, usually at the front, where services are led and where the rabbi speaks.

Bris [sounds like it is spelled]

The ceremony of circumcision and its accompanying reception.

Chalav Yisrael [khah-lahv yis-ra-ael]

Milk or products containing milk where a religious Jew was either directly involved with milking the cow or oversaw the processing.

Challah [khah-luh]

A kneaded loaf of bread, eaten at the start of a Shabbos or Yomtiv meal.

Chametz [khuh-mitz]

1. Food or products containing a mixture of wheat and water which are forbidden to be eaten during Passover.

2. Term loosely used to mean anything forbidden to be eaten or used during Passover.

Channukkah [khah-noo-kuh]

Winter holiday which celebrates the Maccabees' victory over the ancient Greeks and the rededication of the Temple after this miraculous victory. Even more known is the celebration of the miracle of the small jar of pure olive oil which burned for eight days instead of one. Channukkah is *not a* Jewish Christmas, which some unknowing people have a misconception that it is, even though in some years, it happens to coincide with Christmas.

Chasid [khuh-sid]; plural, Chasidim

Members of various sects of Jews who believe in mystical teachings and follow a specific leader, or Rebbe. Chasidic movements originated in Eastern Europe during the 18th century.

Chassnah [khahs–nah]
Hebrew for *wedding*.

Chatzos [khuht–zose]
Jewish noon, or midday.

Chazzan [khah–zahn]
1. A cantor.
2. The person called upon to lead services in the synagogue.

Chevra Kadisha [khev–ruh kuh–dish–uh]
The group of men or women within the Jewish community who prepare Jewish dead for burial: men for men, and women for women.

Chol Hamoed [khohl ha–mo–ed]
The days between the first two and last two days of Pesach and Sukkos.

Cholent [cho–lent]
(There are multiple spellings of this word and various ways to pronounce it.)
A stew–like dish made from meat, potatoes, beans, barley, and other vegetables, usually eaten for Shabbos lunch, having been heated overnight from before the start of Shabbos.

Chumash [khuh–mish]
Same as Torah Definition 1.

Chutzpa [khuhtz–puh]
A daring amount of pure nerve.

Daven [dah–vin]; davenning
To pray; the act of praying.

Devar Torah [de–var to–ruh]
A speech given by an individual discussing any aspect of Torah study.

Eichah [ay–khuh]
The Book of *Lamentations*. Read on the night and following morning of Tisha B'Av.

Ein Kelokaynu [ain ke–lo–kay–noo]
A short prayer, usually sung as a hymn, which occurs just after Musaf. In some traditions, it is recited on a daily basis. The prayer emphasizes no being greater than God.

Eishes Chayil [ay–shes khah–yil]
1. The concluding chapter of the biblical book of *Proverbs*, which discusses the characteristics that are valuable for a woman to have as a wife. Usually sung on Friday night just before Kiddush.
2. A special and beloved woman within the Jewish community.

Eretz Yisrael [eh–retz yis–ra–el]
Hebrew for *The Land of Israel*. The country of Israel.

Erev [eh–rev]
Hebrew for *evening*. The day preceding an important

Jewish calendar day or festival. E.g., Friday is Erev Shabbos. The day before Rosh Hashannah is Erev Rosh Hashannah.

Eruv [ay–ruv, ay–riv, or eh–ruv]

1. An enclosure within which observers of Shabbos can carry objects without violating the restriction against doing so on Shabbos.

2. Often: *Eruv Tavshilin [eh–ruv tahv-shih-lin]* Two foods permitted to be eaten which are set aside with a prayer on the day preceding a festival that will end on Shabbos, so that cooking may take place on Friday for Shabbos.

Fleishig [flay–shig or flay–shik]

Meat foods or foods containing meat, and utensils used in preparation and eating such foods.

Frum [fruhm]

1. Yiddish. Religious; observant.

2. Word used to describe a person or people as being fully observant of all aspects of Jewish law.

Gefilte fish [geh–fil–tuh]

Usually white fish or pike, which is taken whole and ground, so that having to filet it is not necessary. Often, in modern times, the fish is mixed with other ingredients such as matzah meal to make it more commercially appealing.

Gemara [geh–mah–ruh]

Part of the Talmud. Sayings and stories to further interpret the Mishna (See *Mishna.*) Text from which Jewish Law was decided by ancient and modern rabbis.

Glatt [glaht]

With regard to meat, a high standard of kosher supervision that ensures there are absolutely no disqualifying defects in the animal's lungs.

Haftara [hahf–tahrah]

A portion from the books of the *Prophets*, which has a direct connection to the Torah reading or theme of the day, read immediately following the Torah on Shabbos, Yomtiv, and at Minchah on fast days.

Hagafen [hah–guh–fen]

Loosely used to mean the blessing recited over wine.

Haggaddah [huh–guh–duh]

A book used for participating in a Passover Seder. The book contains a description of elements of the story of the Exodus as told at the Seder, as well as the ceremonial instructions, prayers, psalms, and songs.

Halacha [huh–lah–khuh] [hah–lah–khah]

Jewish Law.

Hallel [hah–layl] [hah–lel]

Psalms 113–118, recited on most holidays and Rosh Chodesh, and also as part of the Seder.

Hamotzi
Blessing over bread.

Hashem [huh–shem]
1. God.
2. Hebrew term meaning *the Name.* Used as a substitute for God's name.

Havdallah [huhv–duh–luh] [hahv–dah–lah]
The ceremony which marks the end of Shabbos or Yomtiv. A cup of wine, a candle, and spices are used. At the end of Shabbos, biblical verses of hope are recited. Blessings are recited over the wine, spices, and candle except at the end of Yomtiv, when only wine is used.

Hechshur [hekh–shur]
1. One of several signs printed on packages or containers of food, which denotes that the product in question is certified kosher by one of several reliable rabbinical organizations.
2. The rabbi or rabbinical organization that certifies these products.

Hilchas Shabbos [hil–khas shah–bis]
The laws of Shabbos.

Hoshannah Rabbah [ho–shuh–nuh rah–bah]
The last day of Chol Hamoed Sukkos, on which many processions are made around the lectern in the synagogue and a number of supplicatory prayers are said.

Kabalas Shabbos [kah–buh–lahs shoh–bis]

Literally, welcoming Shabbos. This consists of *Psalms 95–99*, *Psalm 29*, a prayer and hymn, *Psalms 92–93*, and other customary readings.

Kaddish [kaah–dish]

A prayer of sanctification recited in the synagogue, only when a minyan is present. Most important is the mourner's Kaddish, recited by a mourner.

Kiddush [kid–dish] [kee–doosh]

1. A prayer of sanctification recited over a glass of wine, recited on Shabbos and Yomtiv evening and noon, just prior to eating a meal.

2. A reception or meal following morning services on Shabbos or Yomtiv in the synagogue, which begins with the recital of this prayer.

Kinos [kee–nose] or Kinot [kee–note]

Poetry that laments the destruction of the Temple and other misfortunes of Jewish history, recited on the night and morning of Tisha B'Av while sitting on the floor.

Kishka [kish–kuh]

1. Yiddish for *intestine*.

2. A stuffing–like delicacy made from flour, matzah meal, water, fat, and spices. At one time, this was used to stuff cow intestines.

Klal Yisrael [klahl yis–ra–el]

Hebrew for *All of Israel*; all Jews.

Kolel [kol–lel]

A group of newly married and/or newly ordained Orthodox rabbis who further their learning for a few years or learn permanently under the guidance of a leading rabbi.

Kol Nidrei [kole nid–ray]

A recitation which marks the start of prayers on Yom Kippur Night. It consists of a declaration of annulment of vows, and is recited three times by the chazzan or cantor.

Kosher [koe–sher]

1. [Usually:] Food: Any food or food products which are permissible for Jews to eat in accordance with biblical and rabbinic dietary laws.

2. Concept: Being ritually fit for use.

Kotel [koe–tel]

The Western Wall of the Holy Jewish Temple in Jerusalem. It is the only standing remnant of the Temple which has lasted until today. Also known to many as the Wailing Wall.

Kreplach [krep–lokh]

A Jewish delicacy, similar to wonton, which is often eaten just before Yom Kippur and on Purim.

Kugel [koo–gel]

A variety of stuffing–like dishes, including potato, noodle, and carrot. Usually served as a side dish on Shabbos or Yomtiv.

Kumzits [koom–zits]

Yiddish for *come sit.* A gathering of Jews in which people sit (often on the floor) and sing songs and give Torah–oriented speeches.

Lechah Dodi [luh–khah doe–dee]

A joyous hymn which is sung or recited on Friday night during welcoming Shabbos, particularly the figurative Shabbos Queen.

Leining [lain–ing]

The chanting of the Torah and other scriptural readings in the synagogue.

Levi [lay–vee or leh–vee]

A direct descendant of the biblical patriarch Jacob's third son, Levi. Known as a Levite.

Lubavitch [lu–buh–vitch]

The most common Chasidic movement in the world today. Its prime focus is outreach to other Jews.

Lubavitcher [lu–buh–vitch–er]

A follower of this Chasidic movement.

Maariv [mah–riv] [my–riv] [mah–ah–reev]

The evening service. Usually but not always recited after nightfall, except on Friday night.

Machzor [mokh–zer]

A special prayer book for a specific holiday, usually Rosh Hashannah and Yom Kippur.

Mashgiach [mosh–gee–yokh]

1. A person (often a rabbi) who oversees the activities in a kitchen or with food production to make sure that food remains kosher.

2. A Jewish religious ritual supervisor.

Mashiach [muh–she–yokh]

The Jewish Messiah, who, according to Jewish tradition, has not yet come.

Matzah [mah–tzuh] or matzoh

Unleavened bread made from flour and water. It is eaten on Passover to commemorate the Exodus from Egypt, when the Israelites were forced to flee with unbaked dough on their backs.

Matzah balls

A Jewish delicacy similar to dumplings. Balls made from matzah meal, eggs, oil, salt, and water, usually boiled and eaten with chicken soup.

Matzah meal

Ground matzah. On Passover, any type of flour used must come from matzah itself. Therefore, matzah is crushed back into a usable flour–like substance that can be reused for cooking and baking. Matzah meal is used throughout the rest of the year as well.

Mechitza [muh–kheetz–uh]

A separation barrier, usually a movable wall or screen, used to separate men and women in Orthodox synagogues.

Megillah [meh–gil–luh]
1. The Megillah is the biblical book of *Esther*, read in the synagogue on the night and day of Purim.
2. Hebrew for *scroll*.
3. Slang: A long and sometimes unnecessary story.

Melave Malka [mih–lahv–ah mahl–kuh]
A snack or meal eaten on Saturday night, as a symbol of saying goodbye to the figurative Sabbath Queen.

Mezonos [meh–zone–os] or Mezonot
Blessing recited over all foods with the exception of actual bread whose main ingredient is a form of grain.

Mezuman [meh–zoo–min]
An occurrence of three Jewish men who have eaten a meal together and who have begun this meal by washing for bread. In some cases, women make a Mezuman also, although that is not as common.

Mezuzah [meh–zuh–zah]
A thin scroll of parchment which contains *Deuteronomy* 6:4–9 and 11:13–21, usually covered with a plastic, metal, or wooden case, and attached to the doorposts of a Jewish home, dwelling, or institution. There are necklaces and other devices with jewelry attached which are also called mezuzah.

Mikve [mik–vuh], also mikvah
A pool of pure water, usually largely composed of rain water, which is used for ritual purification of one's body or

new dishes which will be owned by observant Jews.

Milchig [mil–khig or mil–khik]

Dairy food or food containing milk and the utensils used to prepare and eat such foods.

Minchah [min–khuh]

Afternoon service. Often, but not always, recited near sunset.

Minyan [min–yin]

A quorum of 10 Jewish males over 13 years of age, needed to serve as the base of a congregation. The Torah cannot be read from a scroll, and many prayers cannot be said, without a minyan present in the synagogue.

Mi Shebayrach [mee sheh–bay–rokh]

(As it relates to our story:) A prayer said for a sick person, asking God for their healing—usually recited in front of the Torah during its reading, usually on Shabbos or Yomtiv.

Mishna [mish–nuh]; plural, Mishnayot

1. Part of the Talmud. Ancient great Jewish sages' interpretation of the Bible set forth as a matter of decrees, rulings, parables, and sayings.

2. A single one of the above.

Mishna Taanis [taa–nis or ta–anit]

The tractate of the Mishna which deals with the laws of fast days.

Mitzvah [mitz–vuh]
1. Hebrew. Literally, a Torah commandment.
2. Loosely defined, a good deed or good turn.

Mitzvos [mitz–vose], also Mitzvot
1. Literally, the 613 commandments that a Jew must follow, also including later rulings by the rabbis.
2. Loosely defined, good deeds.

Modeh Ani [mo–deh ah–nee]
A two-line recitation of thanks, void of God's name, which is said by observant Jews upon awakening, thanking God for restoring one's soul.

Mogetz [muh–gitz]
A Chasidic movement best known for their various melodies.

Musaf [moo–sahf]
An additional service, added onto the morning service, which commemorates the special Shabbos or holiday offering brought to the Temple on that day.

Musar [muh–ser]
Words of rebuke.

Negelvassar [neh–gil–vasser or ney–gil–vasser]
A prescribed ritual handwashing, usually done with a special two-handled cup. It is done before eating bread, first thing in the morning, and at other times when purifying the hands is required.

Netilas You'dayim [not-tee-las you-die-yim,] also Netilat You'dayim

The blessing recited immediately following washing the hands in the morning and before eating bread.

Pareve [parv or par-veh]

Food or food mixtures containing neither dairy nor meat, which may be consumed with or after eating either dairy or meat.

Pesach [pay-sokh or pes-sakh]

Hebrew for *Passover.*

Pesukei Dezimrah [peh-soo-kay dih-zim-ruh]

A collection of Psalms and other biblical passages which are recited as the start of the morning prayers.

Pogrom [poe-grum]

Russian word meaning *destruction.* Massive uprisings against Jews in Eastern Europe in which Jews were killed or forced out of their communities.

Purim [pooh-rim]

The holiday which celebrates the Jews' deliverance from Haman in Persia. Usually occurs sometime in March.

Rabbi

Jewish clergy. Qualified teacher who fronts a Jewish congregation, organization, or other body of Jews.

Rebbe [reb-be]

1. A leader of a Chasidic movement.

2. A teacher or administrator at a Yeshiva.

Rosh Chodesh [roash khoa-desh]

The first day of the new Hebrew month. In some months, it begins with the 30th day of the preceding month.

Rosh Hashannah [roash huh-shuh-nuh]

The Jewish New Year; the first two days of the Jewish year. It is the day when all humanity is judged by God.

Rosh Yeshiva [roash yeh-sheee-vuh]

The head or leading rabbi of a Yeshiva. (See *Yeshiva*.)

Ruach [roo-akh]

1. Festive spirit brought on by religious fervor involving singing and dancing.

2. An element of a person's spirit.

3. Hebrew for *wind* or *spirit*.

Seder [say-der]

1. Usually: Ceremony and meal held on the first two nights of Passover. The story of the Exodus is recounted and discussed.

2. Loosely used: An order of daily learning.

Sefira [seh-fee-ra or so-fee-rah]

Hebrew for *counting*. The period of time lasting from the second night of Passover until the start of Shavuos, when there is a nightly count of each day. During two possible sets of 33 days of this time, haircuts, shaving, weddings, and listening to live music are forbidden. Many also discourage listening to recorded music.

Selichos [slee-khose] or Selichot
Prayers of repentance recited in the days leading up to and during the High Holy Day season. Also recited on public fast days.

Shabbos [shah-bis] or Shabbat [shah-bot]
The Jewish Sabbath, starting from 18 minutes before sunset Friday evening and lasting until various lengths of time on Saturday night.

Shabbaton [shah-bah-toan]
Usually, a large gathering of people who spend part or all of Shabbos together, usually in conjunction with a particular event.

Shacharis [shah-khah-rees] or Shacharit
The morning service.

Shalach Manos [shah-lokh mah-nose] or Shalach Manot
Plates, baskets, or packages of food which observant Jews give to each other on Purim.

Shalom Alaychem [shah-lome ah-lay-khem]
1. Song sung at the start of the first meal of Shabbos, in order to greet visiting angels.
2. Friendly greeting meaning "Peace unto you," said by one Jew when meeting another.

Shaloshudos [shah-lih-shoo-dis]
The third and final meal of Shabbos, usually eaten

around sunset on Shabbos, and lasting until the end of Shabbos.

Shatnes [shaht–nayz]
A forbidden mixture of wool and linen in the same garment, mentioned in *Leviticus* and *Deuteronomy*.

Shavuos [sh'voo–is or sha–voo–is], also Shavuot
The Feast of Weeks. Loosely defined as Pentecost.

Shechinah [sh'khee–nah]
Divine godly spiritual spark.

Shechita [sh'khee–tah]
Kosher slaughter of birds and animals.

Shehakol [sheh–hah–kole]
The blessing recited over any food or beverage other than grain, fruit, vegetables, or wine. Probably the most common blessing over food.

She'ila [shie–luh]
An important question asked of a high–level rabbi concerning circumstances of the law.

Shema [sh'maah]
The Jewish declaration of faith, consisting of *Deuteronomy* 6:4–9 and 11:13–21 and *Numbers* 15:37–41. Recited morning and night as well as at bedtime and when one is certain they are about to die.

Shemoneh Esrei [sh'mo-neh es-ray]

On weekdays, the central prayer of the morning, afternoon, and evening services, consisting of 19 blessings and a concluding meditation.

Shevah Brachos [sheh-vah brah-khose]

1. Hebrew for *the seven blessings*. Seven blessings that are recited at the conclusion of a traditional Jewish wedding ceremony. These same blessings are recited at the end of bensching at the conclusion of the wedding feast, and at the conclusion of feasts throughout the week which follow a wedding.

2. A party which is held within the seven days of rejoicing for the bride and groom, at which these blessings are recited at the end of the meal.

Shiur [she-uhr]

Hebrew for *a measurement*. A lesson. Usually, a Torah-oriented lesson given by a rabbi or learned person.

Shiva [shih-vah]

The first seven days following a funeral, during which immediate relatives of the deceased sit on the floor in their house and are restricted from most activities. Men come to pray with the mourners and both men and women come to visit and comfort the mourners.

Shiva Asar B'Tammuz [she-vuh ah-sar b'tah-muze]

The 17th day of the Hebrew month of Tammuz, which starts the Three Weeks of Mourning. The day is observed as a fast day and five atrocities are remembered, including

Moses breaking the first set of tablets, the daily sacrifices being stopped prior to the destruction of the Second Temple, and a breach being made in the Temple gate.

Shkiah [shkee–ah]
   Sunset.

Shukel [shuh–kul]
   A swinging or swaying movement that an Orthodox Jewish man makes when concentrating on prayer.

Shofar [sho–fir or sho–far]
   Ram's horn, blown on Rosh Hashannah and the conclusion of Yom Kippur. It is also blown following Shacharis for 28 days preceding Rosh Hashannah.

Shomer Shabbos [sho–mehr shah–bis]
   A person or group that is fully observant of and keeps all obligatory laws of Shabbos and Yomtiv.

Shul [shule]
   (Yiddish) Synagogue

Siddur [sid–dir or see–duhr]; plural, Siddurim
   Prayer book.

Simcha [sim–khah]; plural, Simchas
   Hebrew for *joy*. Usually, a joyous occasion.

Simchas Torah [sim–khas torah or simchat torah]
   The last festival day of the autumn holiday season, which celebrates the conclusion of the yearly cycle of

reading the Torah in the synagogue.

S'udah [soo-dah]

A meal which begins with washing for bread.

Sukkah [suh-kah]

Hebrew for *booth*. A temporary structure with tree matter for a roof, constructed outside a Jewish house or building, and used for dining and other living activities during the festival of Sukkos.

Sukkos [suh-kose] or Sukkot [suh-kot]

Literally, the Feast of Booths. Autumn festival of Biblical origin which celebrates the harvest and concentrates on the commandment of dwelling in the Sukkah.

Techum Shabbos [teh-khoom shah-bis]

A distance away from civilization that a person is permitted to walk on Shabbos, about 3,000 feet.

Tefilas Haderech [t'fee-lahs hah-deh-rekh]

Brief traveler's prayer recited at the start of a lengthy journey.

Tefillin [t'fil-lin]

Jewish mens' phylacteries, preferably worn in conjunction with Shacharis. They consist of two leather boxes with straps attached, one for the arm and one for the head, containing four Torah passages.

Tikun [tee-kune]

An all-night session of learning, usually held in the synagogue the first night of Shavuos. The word *Tikun* means correction. A Tikun is held as a correction of the mistake of the Israelites who slept the night before they were to receive the Law on Mount Sinai.

The Three Weeks

Annual period of Jewish mourning in the summer, from the 17th day of the Hebrew month of Tammuz until the day after the ninth of Av (see Tisha B'Av). It occurs anywhere from the last week of June through the beginning of the fourth week of July. The Three Weeks commemorate atrocities of times past, most notably the destruction of both Holy Temples. The last nine and a half days of this period are known as the Nine Days.

Tisha B'Av [tish-ah b'uv]

Fast of the ninth day of the Hebrew month of Av. The day commemorates the destruction of both Holy Temples, the expulsion of Jews from Spain and England, and other tragedies that occurred on this day.

Torah [toe-ruh or toe-ra]

1. The first five books of the Old Testament. Also known as the Five Books of Moses. The five books are: *Genesis*, *Exodus*, *Leviticus*, *Numbers*, and *Deuteronomy*. The cornerstone of Judaism.

2. A scroll made from wood and parchment containing the above in Hebrew, read three times a week and on holidays in the synagogue.

3. Loosely used to mean any educative body of Judaic literature.

Treif [trafe]
Food which is absolutely not kosher.

Tzitzis or Tzitzit [tzih–tzis, tzee–tzeet]
Prayer shawl worn by observant Jewish men. Made of cotton, wool, or other material, having four corners with a fringe on each one. Strings and knots on the fringes serve as a reminder of the 613 commandments, mentioned in *Numbers* and *Deuteronomy*.

Tzom Gedaliah [tzome gih–dahl–yah]
Fast day which occurs the day after Rosh Hashanah, commemorating the death of the last Jewish governor before the remnant of people were sent to Babylon.

Upshirin [up–shee–rin]
Observed by many, this custom involves not cutting a newborn son's hair until or after his third Hebrew birthday. At that time, he is presented with his first yarmulke and first pair of tzitzis.

Vidui [vee–doo–ee]
A confessional prayer which recounts all possible sins; it is part of Selichos.

Yad [yod]
Hebrew for *hand*. Usually, a small instrument with a wooden shaft and metal tip, used by the person currently reading a Torah scroll to keep the place.

Yaakov [ya–ah–kove]
The Hebrew name Jacob.

Yarmulke [yah–mihl–kuh]
Also known as a *kipa*. A round skullcap of varying sizes, usually used by Jewish boys and men as a head covering.

Yarzeit [yahr–tzite]
The anniversary of a Jew's death on the Hebrew calendar. Usually observed by reciting Kaddish in the synagogue and lighting a special candle which burns for up to 24 hours during the entire night and day involved.

Yerushalayim (yeh–roo–shuh–lie–yim]
Hebrew, Jerusalem.

Yeshiva [yeh–shee–vuh or yih–shee–vuh]
An Orthodox Jewish day-school or seminary where the heavier focus is on Jewish learning.

Yiddishkeit [yid–dish–kite]
Orthodox Jewish observances.

Yom Ha'atzmaut [yome hah–ahtz–ma–oot]
Israeli Independence Day. The day on the Hebrew calendar when the State of Israel gained full independence as a country.

Yom Kippur [yome kip–per]
The Jewish Day of Atonement. The holiest day of the year.

Yomtiv [yom–tiv]

Yiddish. A major festival day on which no work may be done. Specifically, Rosh Hashanah, Yom Kippur, the first two days of Sukkos, Shemini Atzeres and Simchas Torah, the first two and last two days of Pesach, and Shavuos.

Zemiros [z'mee–rose], also Zmirot [zmee–rote]

Table hymns sung by many Orthodox Jews on Shabbos.

About the Author

Chaim B. Segal has lived most of his life in Ohio, primarily in the Dayton area. He currently resides in Kettering, Ohio, with his wife, Brooke ("Hava"); their cat, Hanuka; and Chaim's fourth Seeing Eye dog, Yahtzee. Chaim's older brother Moshe and his wife, Hadar, live quite near Chaim and Brooke. The two couples enjoy getting together frequently.

Chaim's late father, Leon, taught at Central State University for 18 years, and also worked as a consultant psychologist for Project Cure, Dayton, Ohio's substance-abuse recovery center. He died in 2003. Chaim's mother, Jane, currently resides at Singing Woods, a senior care facility in north Dayton.

Chaim has enjoyed writing as a hobby since his adolescence, but this is his first book. Other interests include cooking and baking, recording and mixing music, and traveling to new places when time and finances allow for it. He enjoys listening to highly diverse styles of music.

He has nearly 18 years of experience in customer service, and has been employed in this capacity at three jobs, including nearly 12 years working for CSD USA Relay as a communications assistant for the deaf.

Through his writing of *The Sayzeh Song*, as well as other planned works of fiction and nonfiction, he hopes to promote global understanding concerning cultural diversity. He feels that xenophobia is one of our country's worst problems and wishes to promote better understanding among people. His goals include pursuing higher education and eventually working in the area of rehabilitation services.

Contact Information

Email: chaimsegal1968@gmail.com

Cell phone: 937-231-6119

Website: http://www.dvorkin.com/chaimsegal/

March 2016

Editing and Publishing Assistance

This book was proofread and edited by David and Leonore Dvorkin, of Denver, Colorado. David Dvorkin did the cover layout, the formatting and layout of the manuscript, and the publication of the book in e–book and print formats.

David and Leonore are both much–published authors, with more than 30 books (both fiction and nonfiction) and many articles and essays to their credit. Almost all of their books are available for purchase on Amazon, Apple, Barnes & Noble, and other online buying sites in e–book and print formats. A few are in audio format and available from Audible.com.

David's most recent nonfiction book is *DUST NET: The Future of Surveillance, Privacy, and Communication: Why Drones are Just the Beginning* (© 2013).

Leonore's memoir, *Another Chance at Life: A Breast Cancer Survivor's Journey,* is available in both English and Spanish. Both are © 2012. The English edition is also in audio format.

For details, please see their websites:
David Dvorkin: www.dvorkin.com
Leonore H. Dvorkin: www.leonoredvorkin.com

29966616R00124

Made in the USA
Middletown, DE
09 March 2016